The Logic
of the
Moral Sciences

The Logic
of the
Moral Sciences

John Stuart Mill

with an introduction by
A.J. Ayer

Open ❄ Court
La Salle, Illinois

OPEN COURT and the above logo are registered in the U.S. Patent and Trademark Office.

Published by arrangement with Gerald Duckworth & Co. Ltd., London.

Introduction and editorial arrangement © 1987 by Gerald Duckworth & Co., Ltd.

First printing 1988
Second printing 1990
Third printing 1994

Printed and bound in the United States of America.

Library of Congress Cataloging-in-Publication Data

Mill, John Stuart, 1806–1873.
  {On the logic of the moral sciences}
  The logic of the moral sciences/John Stuart Mill; with an introduction by A.J. Ayer.
      p.   cm.
      Originally published as "Book VI. On the logic of the moral sciences" in Mill's A system of logic, ratiocinative and inductive. 8th ed. London: Longmans, Green, Reader, and Dyer, 1872.
      ISBN 0-8126-9005-9 ISBN 0-8126-9053-2 (pbk.)
      1. Ethics 2. Logic. I. Title
  B1603.05 1988
  170--dc19   87-34565
                                                         CIP

Contents

Publisher's Note

This book is a reprint of the Sixth Book of Mill's *A System of Logic ratiocinative and inductive, being a connected view of the principles of evidence and the methods of scientific investigation*, first published in 1843. The text has been reset from the eighth edition (1872), the last edition published in Mill's lifetime.

Introduction

If 'the proper study of mankind is man', it is curious that men of science have done so little to promote it, compared with the progress that they have made in the study of other organisms and in that of the inanimate parts of nature. This discrepancy has grown less in recent years, thanks to the advances made in the domains of human physiology and genetics. In 1843, when John Stuart Mill devoted the sixth and final book of his *A System of Logic* to a disquisition 'On the Logic of the Moral Sciences', it was still very great. Empiricist philosophers of the seventeenth and eighteenth centuries, like John Locke and David Hume, had, indeed, aspired to inaugurate a science of man which would stand comparison with the chemistry and physics of Boyle and Newton, but for all their philosophical acumen, the contributions which they made to political theory and the acuteness of many of Hume's remarks about the passions, they did not leave a legacy on which the social sciences could capitalise. The impression which they had given was that the way to progress lay in the exploration of the principles which governed the association of our ideas, but the attempt made in the early nineteenth century by such men as David Hartley and James Mill, John Stuart Mill's father, to develop this 'associationist psychology' in a systematic fashion had achieved nothing of substantial importance. To all appearances one could learn more about human nature by reading history or even fiction than by trying to subject it to the discipline of science.

This was not a conclusion which John Stuart Mill was willing to accept, at least if it was taken to imply that the application of scientific method to human thought and action was subject to any limitation of principle. He believed that all natural phenomena were governed by universal laws, so that the operations of men's minds were no exception. Not only that, but he believed that the psychological laws in question were discoverable, and even, it would seem, that they were not especially difficult to discover. In his view, the principal reason why the moral had lagged behind the natural sciences was not that men's thoughts and feelings and motives in any way escaped the rule of law, but that the 'ultimate' laws which they obeyed were excessively remote from their concrete instances. The source of this remoteness was not only the number and variety of the 'minor causes' which joined with the major causes in producing specific effects, but also the vast quantity of particular facts which went to determine how even the conjunction of major with minor causes operated in detail. Indeed, at one point, Mill goes so far as to say that nothing which has ever happened to a person is 'without its portion of influence'. The result, since we can never take account of all the relevant factors, is that the generalisations on which we rely 'for predicting phenomena in the concrete' will never be more than approximately true: and so long as they are approximately true, it would not seem to matter whether they are prized out of works of literature or obtained from controlled experiments, which have, as Mill himself acknowledges, a very limited reach in this domain. Nevertheless he thinks it both important and feasible to connect these approximate generalisations 'with the laws of nature from which they result'. Not only is this a necessary condition for our possessing a science of human nature, but it should have the practical advantage of enabling us to make our approximate generalisations cover a larger range of circumstances, and so increase our success in predicting future experience.

It is interesting to note that Mill, who is often accused of underestimating the part that the deductive procedure of framing hypotheses and testing their consequences plays in the natural sciences, maintains that 'The Social Science ... (which, by a convenient barbarism, has been termed Sociology) is a deductive science; not, indeed, after the model of geometry, but after that of the more complex physical sciences.' It might be thought that the model of geometry was obviously inapplicable, but here we must remember that Mill regarded all mathematical propositions as empirical generalisations: his reason for thinking that geometry was not a suitable model for social science was that it allowed no room for 'the case of conflicting forces'; the mistake made by those who took it as a model was that of supposing that social phenomena could

be deduced from a single principle. Since Mill passes for being a
Utilitarian in moral philosophy, it is again interesting to note that he
finds the most remarkable example of this error in the attempt made
by Jeremy Bentham and his followers to base a theory of government
on the single premise 'that men's actions are always determined by
their interests'. Mill points out that it is just not true 'that the actions
even of average rulers are wholly, or anything approaching to wholly,
determined by their personal interest, or even by their own opinion of
their personal interest', and that it is still further from being a
universal truth that the rulers' 'sense of an identity of interest with
the community' is uniquely the effect of their being held responsible
to those whom they govern. This is not to decry the system of
representative government, which Mill himself advocated, but
merely to object to its merits being attributed to a single false
premiss. Mill does not refer to Karl Marx, but there is no doubt that
he would have raised a similar objection to the use of the notion of
class conflict as the universal explanation of historical change.

The geometrical method being excluded, there remain what Mill
calls the Physical and the Historical methods, each of which can,
under the appropriate conditions, yield trustworthy results. The
difference between them is that in the physical method we try to
verify, by observation, hypotheses which we have derived from a
mixture of what we take to be the laws of human nature with an
evaluation of the circumstances which affect their operation in some
particular branch of human activity. The historical method proceeds,
as it were, inversely. It starts with rough generalisations suggested
by the lessons of history. These generalisations would acquire the
status of empirical laws if we were able to deduce them from
psychological laws or from the laws of Ethology, which is Mill's
name for the 'Science of the Formation of Character'. In practice,
this will not be possible, because there are more factors at work than
we are able to reckon with, but we way hope to show that the success
of the generalisations, in the cases under review, is at least a likely
outcome of the dominant laws. There is thus a double process of
verification; the proof, so far as we can achieve it, that our historical
generalisations conform to the laws of human nature, and once
again the observational tests.

Because the explanations of social phenomena are so complex, we
have usually to be content with the Historical method, but there are

cases in which the stronger Physical method can be used. They are those in which a form of human activity functions almost as a separate department within the whole body of social science. An example is Political Economy, which can show what actions would result if men's principal object were the acquisition of wealth. This is by no means always the case, but it covers a wide enough field for the science to yield general consequences from which, if we proceed with the proper caution, we can derive a reasonable number of successful predictions.

It is to be remarked that Mill does not think that his famous inductive methods are applicable to the social sciences. He conjoins them in this book under the slightly odd heading of the Chemical Method. There is the overall difficulty that the subject matter is such as to afford us little or no opportunity for making artificial experiments. We have to rely on the 'spontaneous instances' with which history naturally provides us, and they do not supply the conditions which are requisite for any of the divisions of the Chemical Method to be fruitful. The Method of Difference, preferred by Mill to all others obliges us to find an instance of a phenomenon and one of its absence which are the same in every respect except one, which occurs only in the presence of the phenomenon; and plainly this is a condition that is not historically satisfied. Nor do we fare any better if we resort to what Mill calls the Indirect Method of Difference, where the requirement is that two classes of instances differ only in the one crucial respect. Here too we are defeated by the multiplicity of causes. The same axe falls upon the Method of Agreement, where it is required that two instances of a phenomenon have nothing relevant in common except the circumstance which is our candidate for its cause. To take Mill's own example, let us suppose that we discover a set of prosperous nations which, within the limits of our enquiry, agree only in practising commercial protection. We cannot infer that this common practice is the cause of their prosperity. The reason why we cannot is that we have not proved either that protectionism would in any case be sufficient on its own, or that various combinations of the divergent factors would not yield prosperity even in the absence of protectionism. Similar objections apply to the method of Concomitant Variations, and the Method of Residues presupposes, what is not here the case, that 'the causes from which part of the effect proceeded are already known'. To the extent that they can be known, it must be by deduction from the 'principles of human nature'. But then the Method of Residues becomes superfluous. The use of one or other of the appropriate deductive methods will do its work.

But will it? Or rather, can there be any method that comes anywhere near achieving Mill's objective, the discovery and application of the laws which govern all the acts of men? By what right does he assume that there are such laws? Is it not possible that the mind of man is not, in this sense, a subject for science at all?

The most common reason for denying that man is a legitimate subject for science is his alleged possession of free-will. Mill considers this objection and dismisses it. He does not deny that we possess free-will, in the sense that we have reasons for our actions and act upon them. We are not prisoners of fate, in the sense that the course of our lives proceeds independently of the choices that we make. A man's choices are, indeed, conditioned by his character, but his character is not something that he has no power to alter. The circumstances which form it include his own desires, and one such desire, which can often be realised, is the desire to make himself, in some degree, a different sort of person. In Mill's view 'this feeling, of our being able to modify our own character *if we wish*', is what constitutes our feeling of moral freedom.

None of this, however, is inconsistent with determinism. It remains true, according to Mill, 'that if we knew the person thoroughly, and knew all the inducements which are acting upon him, we could foretell his conduct with as much certainty as we can predict any physical event'. It is simply that his being the sort of person that he is, his consequently having such and such motives, and the manner and degree in which he acts upon these motives, are all matters of fact which fit into a regular pattern, when the attendant circumstances are taken into account: the uniformity of these patterns is captured by the generalisations to which we give the name of natural laws. To say that all human actions are predictable is, thus, to say no more than that with respect to any statement which truly describes a human action there is a set of laws and a set of true statements about the attendant circumstances from the conjunction of which the statement in question follows.

Why then should the thesis of determinism have been so widely seen as robbing us of our pretensions to free-will? Mill's answer is that people have been misled by the improper use of the word 'necessity' to express 'the simple fact of causation'. 'Necessity' suggests constraint. If people are told that they necessarily think and feel and act as they do, they conclude that they are being represented as the helpless prisoners of fate. When it is explained to them that 'necessity' in this context implies no more than 'mere uniformity of sequence', they should cease to feel that their dignity or even their autonomy is threatened.

There is something in this. If a man is said to be acting under constraint only in cases where his choice is not a causal factor, or those in which it is subject to obvious pressures, such as his having a pistol pointed at his head, then the fact that an action is causally explicable does not entail that it is performed under constraint; and if it is only the factor of constraint that removes or greatly diminishes the freedom of the will, we can consistently hold that most human actions are done freely while also holding that they are causally determined. Even so, I doubt if this would be enough to satisfy any fervent believer in the existence of free-will. He would argue that the issue is not merely whether we find ourselves able to realise our choices, but also how we come to make the choices that we do, and if the answer involves a chain of causes which takes us back to our genetic endowment and its responses to external stimuli, over which we have no control, he would conclude that we are not really free. But the trouble with such people is that they are making a demand which cannot possibly be met. They would be no happier with the answer that our choices are ascribable, at least in some degree, to chance. They stand by a concept of self-determination to which no sense can be attached.

This is not to say that the case for determinism in the domain of the social sciences has been made out. The most that can be claimed is that we have no good reason for dismissing it without further enquiry. The likelihood that the laws which govern the behaviour of atomic particles are fundamentally statistical allows room for causal laws to prevail at the macro-level of human thought and conduct. But then we need some proof that they do prevail. We need to discover and apply them successfully. This is not something that we have the right to take for granted *a priori*. To say, as Mill does, that we should be able to predict a person's conduct if only we knew enough about his character and circumstances is nothing more than an encouragement to pursue research, unless the laws which support the predictions are at least roughly specified. The claim will be deprived of content if no amount of failure is allowed to affect it, if, however unsuccessful we are, we protect our thesis by appealing to our lack of knowledge. If we are to proceed scientifically, we must allow our continued failure to light upon causal laws as bestowing at least some probability on the conclusion that they are not discoverable.

In fact 'The Laws of Mind' which Mill himself adduces are certainly not sufficient to generate either of his deductive methods. Apart from the major generalisation, which may not even be true, that every state of consciousness can be reproduced in memory, he relies on three laws of association; first, that similar ideas tend to excite one another; secondly, that where two impressions have frequently occurred in close temporal conjunction, the recurrence or the idea of one of them tends to excite the idea of the other; and, thirdly, that the more intense either or both of the impressions are, the more frequently will this excitement operate. No doubt these generalisations could be given more factual content, but the mass of detail required would appear too great for them to be transformable into manageable laws.

A more promising approach would be to have recourse to physiology. We should need an established theory accounting for the succession of states of the central nervous system, and a set of well-supported hypotheses serving to correlate these states with states of consciousness. Mill allows this to be possible, but dismisses it as impractical, which, indeed, it still remains. For all the advances that have been made in physiology, we are still very far from being able to meet such ambitious demands. We must continue to be content with explaining human conduct in terms of desires and purposes, attributed on the basis of statements of tendency, and arriving at predictions of which the best that can be said is that, so long as they allow for a fair amount of variation in detail, and do not venture very far into the future, they are successful in the main.

There remains the question whether we are able to discover social laws which, like the proportion of male to female births or the expectation of life in a given community, can be taken as holding good, without our having to enquire into the particular facts concerning individual persons on which their truth finally depends. It is widely believed that there are such laws, but the candidates which have been put forward, such as the dependence of social institutions upon economic interests, have at best a limited application. There is also the major difficulty that the cultural and technological developments which play so great a part in all our lives, are, directly or indirectly, the outcome of the work of a few exceptionally gifted men: and even though the birth of such men is subject to the laws of genetics, we cannot make use of these laws or any others at our disposal in order to predict the ways in which these gifts will actually be manifested. It is all very well to say that the social conditions were such that if Newton or Darwin or Mozart or Cezanne had not existed, someone else would have achieved similar results at much the same time. As Mill himself acknowledges, this claim is not supported by anything approaching sufficient evidence. If we confine ourselves, therefore, to what the state of our knowledge reasonably allows us to count as predictable, eschewing idle talk of what might be predicted if only we knew more, we have to conclude that a decisive part in human affairs is played by a factor of chance which we are not, and probably never shall be, in a position to eliminate.

A.J. Ayer

On the Logic of the Moral Sciences

Si l'homme peut prédire, avec une assurance presque entière, les phénomènes dont il connaît les lois; si lors même qu'elles lui sont inconnues, il peut, d'après l'expérience, prévoir avec une grande probabilité les événemens de l'avenir; pourquoi regarderait-on comme une entreprise chimérique, celle de tracer avec quelque vraisemblance le tableau des destinées futures de l'espèce humaine, d'après les résultats de son histoire? Le seul fondement de croyance dans les sciences naturelles, est cette idée, que les lois générales, connues ou ignorées, qui règlent les phénomènes de l'univers, sont nécessaires et constantes; et par quelle raison ce principe serait-il moins vrai pour le développement des facultés intellectuelles et morales de l'homme, que pour les autres opérations de la nature? Enfin, puisque des opinions formées d'après l'expérience ... sont la seule règle de la conduite des hommes les plus sages, pourquoi interdirait-on au philosophe d'appuyer ses conjectures sur cette même base, pourvu qu'il ne leur attribue pas une certitude supérieure à celle qui peut naître du nombre, de la constance, de l'exactitude des observations?

Condorcet, *Esquisse d'un Tableau Historique des Progrès de l'Esprit Humain.*

If man can predict, with almost total confidence, phenomena whose laws he knows, and if, even when they are unknown to him, he can foresee future events with a general probability from experience, why should it be thought fanciful to attempt a sketch of man's future on the evidence of his past? In the natural sciences the only basis of belief is the idea that the general laws, known or unknown, which control the phenomena of the universe are necessary and constant; and why should this principle be any less true for the other workings of nature? Finally, since opinions formed from experience ... are the sole rule of conduct of the wise, why should we not allow the philosopher to base his conjectures on the same foundation, provided that he does not attribute to them a certainty greater than can arise from the number, constancy and accuracy of the observations? (tr. by Colin Haycraft)

CHAPTER ONE

Introductory Remarks

1. The backward state of the moral sciences can only be remedied by applying to them the methods of physical science, duly extended and generalised

Principles of Evidence and Theories of Method are not to be constructed *à priori*. The laws of our rational faculty, like those of every other natural agency, are only learnt by seeing the agent at work. The earlier achievements of science were made without the conscious observance of any Scientific Method; and we should never have known by what process truth is to be ascertained if we had not previously ascertained many truths. But it was only the easier problems which could be thus resolved; natural sagacity, when it tried its strength against the more difficult ones, either failed altogether, or if it succeeded here and there in obtaining a solution, had no sure means of convincing others that its solution was correct. In scientific investigation, as in all other works of human skill, the way of obtaining the end is seen as it were instinctively by superior minds in some comparatively simple case, and is then, by judicious generalisation, adapted to the variety of complex cases. We learn to do a thing in difficult circumstances by attending to the manner in which we have spontaneously done the same thing in easier ones.

This truth is exemplified by the history of the various branches of knowledge which have successively, in the ascending order of their complication, assumed the character of sciences; and will doubtless receive fresh confirmation from those of which the final scientific constitution is yet to come, and which are still abandoned to the uncertainties of vague and popular discussion. Although several other sciences have emerged from this state at a comparatively recent date, none now remain in it except those which relate to man himself, the most complex and most difficult subject of study on which the human mind can be engaged.

Concerning the physical nature of man as an organised being, – though there is still much uncertainty and much controversy, which can only be terminated by the general acknowledgment and employment of stricter rules of induction than are commonly recognised, – there is, however, a considerable body of truths which all who have attended to the subject consider to be fully established; nor is there now any radical imperfection in the method observed in this department of science by its most distinguished modern teachers. But the laws of Mind, and, in even a greater degree, those of Society, are so far from having attained a similar state of even partial recognition, that it is still a controversy whether they are capable of becoming subjects of science in the strict sense of the term; and among those who are agreed on this point there reigns the most irreconcilable diversity on almost every other. Here, therefore, if anywhere, the principles laid down in the preceding Books may be expected to be useful.

If, on matters so much the most important with which human intellect can occupy itself, a more general agreement is ever to exist among thinkers; if what has been pronounced 'the proper study of mankind' is not destined to remain the only subject which Philosophy cannot succeed in rescuing from Empiricism; the same process through which the laws of many simpler phenomena have by general acknowledgment been placed beyond dispute must be consciously and deliberately applied to those more difficult inquiries. If there are some subjects on which the results obtained have finally received the unanimous assent of all who have attended to the proof, and others on which mankind have not yet been equally successful; on which the most sagacious minds have occupied themselves from the earliest date, and have never succeeded in establishing any considerable body of truths, so as to be beyond denial or doubt; it is by generalising the methods successfully followed in the former inquiries, and adapting them to the latter, that we may hope to remove this blot on the face of science. The remaining chapters are an endeavour to facilitate this most desirable object.

2. How far this can be attempted in the present work

In attempting this, I am not unmindful how little can be done towards it in a mere treatise on Logic, or how vague and unsatisfactory all precepts of Method must necessarily appear when not practically exemplified in the establishment of a body of doctrine. Doubtless, the most effectual mode of showing how the sciences of Ethics and Politics may be constructed would be to construct them: a task which, it needs scarcely be said, I am not about to undertake. But even if there were no other examples, the memorable one of Bacon would be sufficient to demonstrate that it is sometimes both possible and useful to point out the way, though without being oneself prepared to adventure far into it. And if more were to be attempted, this at least is not a proper place for the attempt.

In substance, whatever can be done in a work like this for the Logic of the Moral Sciences, has been or ought to have been accomplished in the five preceding Books; to which the present can be only a kind of supplement or appendix, since the methods of investigation applicable to moral and social science must have been already described, if I have succeeded in enumerating and characterising those of science in general. It remains, however, to examine which of those methods are more especially suited to the various branches of moral inquiry; under what peculiar faculties or difficulties they are there employed; how far the unsatisfactory state of those inquiries is owing to a wrong choice of methods, how far to want of skill in the application of right ones; and what degree of ultimate success may be attained or hoped for by a better choice and more careful employment of logical processes appropriate to the case. In other words, whether moral sciences exist, or can exist; to what degree of perfection they are susceptible of being carried; and by what selection or adaptation of the methods brought to view in the previous part of this work that degree of perfection is attainable.

At the threshold of this inquiry we are met by an objection, which, if not removed, would be fatal to the attempt to treat human conduct as a subject of science. Are the actions of human beings, like all other natural events, subject to invariable laws? Does that constancy of causation, which is the foundation of every scientific theory of successive phenomena, really obtain among them? This is often denied; and, for the sake of systematic completeness, if not from any very urgent practical necessity, the question should receive a deliberate answer in this place. We shall devote to the subject a chapter apart.

CHAPTER TWO

Of Liberty and Necessity

1. Are human actions subject to the law of causality?

The question whether the law of causality applies in the same strict sense to human actions as to other phenomena, is the celebrated controversy concerning the freedom of the will, which, from at least as far back as the time of Pelagius, has divided both the philosophical and the religious world. The affirmative opinion is commonly called the doctrine of Necessity, as asserting human volitions and actions to be necessary and inevitable. The negative maintains that the will is not determined, like other phenomena, by antecedents, but determines itself; that our volitions are not, properly speaking, the effects of causes, or at least have no causes which they uniformly and implicitly obey.

I have already made it sufficiently apparent that the former of these opinions is that which I consider the true one; but the misleading terms in which it is often expressed, and indistinct manner in which it is usually apprehended, have both obstructed its reception and perverted its influence when received. The metaphysical theory of free-will, as held by philosophers, (for the practical feeling of it, common in a greater or less degree to all mankind, is in no way inconsistent with the contrary theory,) was invented because the supposed alternative of admitting human actions to be *necessary* was deemed inconsistent with every one's instinctive consciousness, as well as humiliating to the pride, and even degrading to the moral nature, of man. Nor do I deny that the doctrine, as sometimes held, is open to these imputations; for the misapprehension in which I shall be able to show that they originate unfortunately is not confined to the opponents of the doctrine, but is participated in by many, perhaps we might say by most, of its supporters.

2. *The doctrine commonly called philosophical necessity, in what sense true*

Correctly conceived, the doctrine called Philosophical Necessity is simply this: that, given the motives which are present to an individual's mind, and given likewise the character and disposition of the individual, the manner in which he will act might be unerringly inferred; that if we knew the person thoroughly, and knew all the inducements which are acting upon him, we could foretell his conduct with as much certainty as we can predict any physical event. This proposition I take to be a mere interpretation of universal experience, a statement in words of what every one is internally convinced of. No one who believed that he knew thoroughly the circumstances of any case, and the characters of the different persons concerned, would hesitate to foretell how all of them would act. Whatever degree of doubt he may in fact feel arises from the uncertainty whether he really knows the circumstances, or the character of some one or other of the persons, with the degree of accuracy required; but by no means from thinking that if he did know these things, there could be any uncertainty what the conduct would be. Nor does this full assurance conflict in the smallest degree with what is called our feeling of freedom. We do not feel ourselves the less free because those to whom we are intimately known are well assured how we shall will to act in a particular case. We often, on the contrary, regard the doubt what our conduct will be as a mark of ignorance of our character, and sometimes even resent it as an imputation. The religious metaphysicians who have asserted the freedom of the will have always maintained it to be consistent with divine foreknowledge of our actions; and if with divine, then with any other foreknowledge. We may be free, and yet another may have reason to be perfectly certain what use we shall make of our freedom. It is not, therefore, the doctrine that our volitions and actions are invariable consequents of our antecedent states of mind, that is either contradicted by our consciousness or felt to be degrading.

But the doctrine of causation, when considered as obtaining between our volitions and their antecedents, is almost universally conceived as involving more than this. Many do not believe, and very few practically feel, that there is nothing in causation but invariable, certain, and unconditional sequence. There are few to whom mere constancy of succession appears a sufficiently stringent bond of union for so peculiar a relation as that of cause and effect. Even if the reason repudiates, the imagination retains, the feeling of some more intimate connection, of some peculiar tie or mysterious constraint exercised by the antecedent over the consequent. Now this it is which, considered as applying to the human will, conflicts with our consciousness and revolts our feelings. We are certain that, in the case of our volitions, there is not this mysterious constraint. We know that we are not compelled, as by a magical spell, to obey any particular motive. We feel that if we wished to prove that we have the power of resisting the motive, we could do so, (that wish being, it needs scarcely be observed, a *new antecedent*;) and it would be humiliating to our pride, and (what is of more importance) paralysing to our desire of excellence, if we thought otherwise. But neither is any such mysterious compulsion now supposed, by the best philosophical authorities, to be exercised by any other cause over its effect. Those who think that causes draw their effects after them by a mystical tie are right in believing that the relation between volitions and their antecedents is of another nature. But they should go farther, and admit that this is also true of all other effects and their antecedents. If such a tie is considered to be involved in the word necessity, the doctrine is not true of human actions; but neither is it then true of inanimate objects. It would be more correct to say that matter is not bound by necessity, than that mind is so.

That the free-will metaphysicians, being mostly of the school which rejects Hume's and Brown's analysis of Cause and Effect, should miss their way for want of the light which that analysis affords, cannot surprise us. The wonder is, that the Necessitarians, who usually admit that philosophical theory, should in practice equally lose sight of it. The very same misconception of the doctrine called Philosophical Necessity which prevents the opposite party from recognising its truth, I believe to exist more or less obscurely in the minds of most Necessitarians, however they may in words disavow it. I am much mistaken if they habitually feel that the necessity which they recognise in actions is but uniformity of order, and capability of being predicted. They have a feling as if there were at bottom a stronger tie between the volitions and their causes; as if, when they asserted that the will is governed by the balance of motives, they meant something more cogent than if they had only said, that whoever knew the motives, and our habitual susceptibilities to them, could predict how we should will to act. They commit, in opposition to their own scientific system, the very same mistake which their adversaries commit in obedience to theirs; and in consequence do really in some instances suffer those depressing consequences which their opponents erroneously impute to the doctrine itself.

3. Inappropriateness and pernicious effect of the term necessity

I am inclined to think that this error is almost wholly an effect of the associations with a word, and that it would be prevented by forbearing to employ, for the expression of the simple fact of causation, so extremely inappropriate a term as Necessity. That word, in its other acceptations, involves much more than mere uniformity of sequence: it implies irresistibleness. Applied to the will, it only means that the given cause will be followed by the effect, subject to all possibilities of counteraction by other causes; but in common use it stands for the operation of those causes exclusively, which are supposed too powerful to be counteracted at all. When we say that all human actions take place of necessity, we only mean that they will certainly happen if nothing prevents: – when we say that dying of want, to those who cannot get food, is a necessity, we mean that it will certainly happen, whatever may be done to prevent it. The application of the same term to the agencies on which human actions depend as is used to express those agencies of nature which are really uncontrollable, cannot fail, when habitual, to create a feeling of uncontrollableness in the former also. This, however, is a mere illusion. There are physical sequences which we call necessary, as death for want of food or air; there are others which, though as much cases of causation as the former, are not said to be necessary, as death from poison, which an antidote, or the use of the stomach-pump, will sometimes avert. It is apt to be forgotten by people's feelings, even if remembered by their understandings, that human actions are in this last predicament: they are never (except in some cases of mania) ruled by any one motive with such absolute sway that there is no room for the influence of any other. The causes, therefore, on which action depends are never uncontrollable, and any given effect is only necessary provided that the causes tending to produce it are not controlled. That whatever happens could not have happened otherwise unless something had taken place which was capable of preventing it, no one surely needs hesitate to admit. But to call this by the name necessity is to use the term in a sense so different from its primitive and familiar meaning, from that which it bears in the common occasions of life, as to amount almost to a play upon words. The associations derived from the ordinary sense of the term will adhere to it in spite of all we can do; and though the doctrine of Necessity, as stated by most who hold it, is very remote from fatalism, it is probable that most Necessitarians are Fatalists, more or less, in their feelings.

A Fatalist believes, or half believes, (for nobody is a consistent Fatalist,) not only that whatever is about to happen will be the infallible result of the causes which produce it, (which is the true Necessitarian doctrine,) but, moreover, that there is no use in struggling against it; that it will happen however we may strive to prevent it. Now, a Necessitarian, believing that our actions follow from our characters, and that our characters follow from our organisation, our education, and our circumstances, is apt to be, with more or less of consciousness on his part, a Fatalist as to his own actions, and to believe that his nature is such, or that his education and circumstances have so moulded his character, that nothing can now prevent him from feeling and acting in a particular way, or at least that no effort of his own can hinder it. In the words of the sect which in our own day has most perseveringly inculcated and most perversely misunderstood this great doctrine, his character is formed *for* him, and not *by* him; therefore his wishing that it had been formed differently is of no use; he has no power to alter it. But this is a grand error. He has, to a certain extent, a power to alter his character. Its being, in the ultimate resort, formed for him, is not inconsistent with its being, in part, formed *by* him as one of the intermediate agents. His character is formed by his circumstances, (including among these his particular organisation,) but his own desire to mould it in a particular way is one of those circumstances, and by no means one of the least influential. We cannot, indeed, directly will to be different from what we are; but neither did those who are supposed to have formed our characters directly will that we should be what we are. Their will had no direct power except over their own actions. They made us what they did make us by willing, not the end, but the requisite means; and we, when our habits are not too inveterate, can, by similarly willing the requisite means, make ourselves different. If they could place us under the influence of certain circumstances, we in like manner can place ourselves under the influence of other circumstances. We are exactly as capable of making our own character, *if we will*, as others are of making it for us.

Yes, (answers the Owenite,) but these words, 'if we will', surrender the whole point, since the will to alter our own character is given us, not by any efforts of ours, but by circumstances which we cannot help; it comes to us either from external causes or not at all. Most true: if the Owenite stops here, he is in a position from which nothing can expel him. Our character is formed by us as well as for us; but the wish which induces us to attempt to form it is formed for us; and how? Not, in general, by our organisation, nor wholly by our education, but by our experience – experience of the painful consequences of the character we previously had, or by some strong feeling of admiration or aspiration accidentally aroused. But to think that we have no power of altering our characater, and to think that we shall not use our power unless we desire to use it, are very different things, and have a very different effect on the mind. A person who does not wish to alter his character cannot be the person who is supposed to feel discouraged or paralysed by thinking himself unable to do it. The depressing effect of the Fatalist doctrine can only be felt where there *is* a wish to do what that doctrine represents as impossible. It is of no consequence what we think forms our character, when we have no desire of our own about forming it, but it is of great consequence that we should not be prevented from forming such a desire by thinking the attainment impracticable, and that if we have the desire we should know that the work is not so irrevocably done as to be incapable of being altered.

And, indeed, if we examine closely, we shall find that this feeling, of our being able to modify our own character *if we wish*, is itself the feeling of moral freedom which we are conscious of. A person feels morally free who feels that his habits or his temptations are not his masters, but he theirs: who even in yielding to them knows that he could resist; that were he desirous of altogether throwing them off, there would not be required for that purpose a stronger desire than he knows himself to be capable of feeling. It is of course necessary, to render our consciousness of freedom complete, that we should have succeeded in making our character all we have hitherto attempted to make it; for if we have wished and not attained, we have, to that extent, not power over our own character – we are not free. Or at least, we must feel that our wish, if not strong enough to alter our character, is strong enough to conquer our character when the two are brought into conflict in any particular case of conduct. And hence it is said with truth, that none but a person of confirmed virtue is completely free.

The application of so improper a term as Necessity to the doctrine of cause and effect in the matter of human character seems to me one of the most signal instances in philosophy of the abuse of terms, and its practical consequences one of the most striking examples of the power of language over our associations. The subject will never be generally understood until that objectionable term is dropped. The free-will doctrine, by keeping in view precisely that portion of the truth which the word Necessity puts out of sight, namely, the power of the mind to co-operate in the formation of its own character, has given to its adherents a practical feeling much nearer to the truth than has generally (I believe) existed in the minds of Necessitarians. The latter may have had a stronger sense of the importance of what human beings can do to shape the characters of one another; but the free-will doctrine has, I believe, fostered in its supporters a much stronger spirit of self-culture.

4. *A motive not always the anticipation of a pleasure or a pain*

There is still one fact which requires to be noticed (in addition to the existence of a power of self-formation) before the doctrine of the causation of human actions can be freed from the confusion and misapprehensions which surround it in many minds. When the will is said to be determined by motives, a motive does not mean always, or solely, the anticipation of a pleasure or of a pain. I shall not here inquire whether it be true that, in the commencement, all our voluntary actions are mere means consciously employed to obtain some pleasure or avoid some pain. It is at least certain that we gradually, through the influence of association, come to desire the means, without thinking of the end: the action itself becomes an object of desire, and is performed without reference to any motive beyond itself. Thus far, it may still be objected, that the action having through association become pleasurable, we are, as much as before, moved to act by the anticipation of a pleasure, namely, the pleasure of the action itself. But granting this, the matter does not end here. As we proceed in the formation of habits, and become accustomed to will a particular act or a particular course of conduct because it is pleasurable, we at last continue to will it without any reference to its being pleasurable. Although, from some change in us or in our circumstances, we have ceased to find any pleasure in the action, or perhaps to anticipate any pleasure as the consequence of it, we still continue to desire the action, and consequently to do it. In this manner it is that habits of hurtful excess continue to be practised although they have ceased to be pleasurable; and in this manner also it is that the habit of willing to persevere in the course which he has chosen does not desert the moral hero, even when the reward, however real, which he doubtless receives from the consciousness of well-doing, is anything but an equivalent for the sufferings he undergoes or the wishes which he may have to renounce.

A habit of willing is commonly called a purpose; and among the causes of our volitions, and of the actions which flow from them, must be reckoned not only likings and aversions, but also purposes. It is only when our purposes have become independent of the feelings of pain or pleasure from which they originally took their rise that we are said to have a confirmed character. 'A character,' says Novalis, 'is a completely fashioned will'; and the will, once so fashioned, may be steady and constant, when the passive susceptibilities of pleasure and pain are greatly weakened or materially changed.

With the corrections and explanations now given, the doctrine of the causation of our volitions by motives, and of motives by the desirable objects offered to us, combined with our particular susceptibilities of desire, may be considered, I hope, as sufficiently established for the purposes of this treatise.*

---

* Some arguments and explanations, supplementary to those in the text, will be found in *An Examination of Sir William Hamilton's Philosophy*, chap. xxvi.

CHAPTER THREE

That there is, or may be, a Science of Human Nature

1. There may be sciences which are not exact sciences

It is a common notion, or at least it is implied in many common modes of speech, that the thoughts, feelings, and actions of sentient beings are not a subject of science, in the same strict sense in which this is true of the objects of outward nature. This notion seems to involve some confusion of ideas, which it is necessary to begin by clearing up.

Any facts are fitted, in themselves, to be a subject of science, which follow one another according to constant laws; although those laws may not have been discovered, nor even be discoverable by our existing resources. Take, for instance, the most familiar class of meteorological phenomena, those of rain and sunshine. Scientific inquiry has not yet succeeded in ascertaining the order of antecedence and consequence among these phenomena, so as to be able, at least in our regions of the earth, to predict them with certainty or even with any high degree of probability. Yet no one doubts that the phenomena depend on laws, and that these must be derivative laws resulting from known ultimate laws, those of heat, electricity, vaporisation, and elastic fluids. Nor can it be doubted that if we were acquainted with all the antecedent circumstances, we could, even from those more general laws, predict (saving difficulties of calculation) the state of the weather at any future time. Meteorology, therefore, not only has in itself every natural requisite for being, but actually is, a science; though, from the difficulty of observing the facts on which the phenomena depend, (a difficulty inherent in the peculiar nature of those phenomena,) the science is extremely imperfect; and were it perfect, might probably be of little avail in practice, since the data requisite for applying its principles to particular instances would rarely be procurable.

A case may be conceived of an intermediate character between the perfection of science and this its extreme imperfection. It may happen that the greater causes, those on which the principal part of the phenomena depends, are within the reach of observation and measurement; so that if no other causes intervened, a complete explanation could be given not only of the phenomenon in general, but of all the variations and modifications which it admits of. But inasmuch as other, perhaps many other causes, separately insignificant in their effects, co-operate or conflict in many or in all cases with those greater causes, the effect, accordingly, presents more or less of aberration from what would be produced by the greater causes alone. Now if these minor causes are not so constantly accessible, or not accessible at all to accurate observation, the principal mass of the effect may still, as before, be accounted for, and even predicted; but there will be variations and modifications which we shall not be competent to explain thoroughly, and our predictions will not be fulfilled accurately, but only approximately.

It is thus, for example, with the theory of the tides. No one doubts that Tidology (as Dr Whewell proposes to call it) is really a science. As much of the phenomena as depends on the attraction of the sun and moon is completely understood, and may in any, even unknown, part of the earth's surface be foretold with certainty; and the far greater part of the phenomena depends on those causes. But circumstances of a local or casual nature, such as the configuration of the bottom of the ocean, the degree of confinement from shores, the direction of the wind, etc., influence in many or in all places the height and time of the tide; and a portion of these circumstances being either not accurately knowable, not precisely measurable, or not capable of being certainly foreseen, the tide in known places commonly varies from the calculated result of general principles by some difference that we cannot explain, and in unknown ones may vary from it by a difference that we are not able to foresee or conjecture. Nevertheless, not only is it certain that these variations depend on causes, and follow their causes by laws of unerring uniformity; not only, therefore, is tidology a science, like meteorology, but it is what, hitherto at least, meteorology is not, a science largely available in practice. General laws may be laid down respecting the tides; predictions may be founded on those laws, and the result will in the main, though often not with complete accuracy, correspond to the predictions.

And this is what is or ought to be meant by those who speak of sciences which are not *exact* sciences. Astronomy was once a science, without being an exact science. It could not become exact until not only the general course of the planetary motions, but the perturbations also, were accounted for, and referred to their causes. It has become an exact science, because its phenomena have been brought under laws comprehending the whole of the causes by which the phenomena are influenced, whether in a great or only in a trifling degree, whether in all or only in some cases, and assigning to each of those causes the share of effect which really belongs to it. But in the theory of the tides, the only laws at yet accurately ascertained are those of the causes which affect the phenomenon in all cases, and in a considerable degree; while others which affect it in some cases only, or, if in all, only in a slight degree, have not been sufficiently ascertained and studied to enable us to lay down their laws, still less to deduce the completed law of the phenomenon, by compounding the effects of the greater with those of the minor causes. Tidology, therefore, is not yet an exact science; not from any inherent incapacity of being so, but from the difficulty of ascertaining with complete precision the real derivative uniformities. By combining, however, the exact laws of the greater causes, and of such of the minor ones as are sufficiently known, with such empirical laws or such approximate generalisations respecting the miscellaneous variations as can be obtained by specific observation, we can lay down general propositions which will be true in the main, and on which, with allowance for the degree of their probable inaccuracy, we may safely ground our expectations and our conduct.

2. To what scientific type the science of human nature corresponds

The science of human nature is of this description. It falls far short of the standard of exactness now realised in Astronomy; but there is no reason that it should not be as much a science as Tidology is, or as Astronomy was when its calculations had only mastered the main phenomena, but not the perturbations.

The phenomena with which this science is conversant being the thoughts, feelings, and actions of human beings, it would have attained the ideal perfection of a science if it enabled us to foretell how an individual would think, feel, or act throughout life, with the same certainty with which astronomy enables us to predict the places and the occultations of the heavenly bodies. It needs scarcely be stated that nothing approaching to this can be done. The actions of individuals could not be predicted with scientific accuracy, were it only because we cannot foresee the whole of the circumstances in which those individuals will be placed. But further, even in any given combination of (present) circumstances, no assertion, which is both precise and universally true, can be made respecting the manner in which human beings will think, feel, or act. This is not, however, because every person's modes of thinking, feeling, and acting do not depend on causes; nor can we doubt that if, in the case of any individual, our data could be complete, we even now know enough of the ultimate laws by which mental phenomena are determined to enable us in many cases to predict, with tolerable certainty, what, in the greater number of supposable combinations of circumstances, his conduct or sentiments would be. But the impressions and actions of human beings are not solely the result of their present circumstances, but the joint result of those circumstances and of the characters of the individuals; and the agencies which determine human character are so numerous and diversified, (nothing which has happened to the person throughout life being without its portion of influence,) that in the aggregate they are never in any two cases exactly similar. Hence, even if our science of human nature were theoretically perfect, that is, if we could calculate any character as we can calculate the orbit of any planet, *from given data*; still, as the data are never all given, nor ever precisely alike in different cases, we could neither make positive predictions, nor lay down universal propositions.

Inasmuch, however, as many of those effects which it is of most importance to render amenable to human foresight and control are determined, like the tides, in an incomparably greater degree by general causes, than by all partial causes taken together; depending in the main on those circumstances and qualities which are common to all mankind, or at least to large bodies of them, and only to a small degree on the idiosyncrasies of organisation or the peculiar history of individuals; it is evidently possible, with regard to all such effects, to make predictions which will *almost* always be verified, and general propositions which are almost always true. And whenever it is sufficient to know how the great majority of the human race, or of some nation or class of persons, will think, feel, and act, these propositions are equivalent to universal ones. For the purposes of political and social science this *is* sufficient. As we formerly remarked,* an approximate generalisation is, in social inquiries, for most practical purposes equivalent to an exact one; that which is only probable when asserted of individual human beings indiscriminately selected, being certain when affirmed of the character and collective conduct of masses.

It is no disparagement, therefore, to the science of Human Nature that those of its general propositions which descend sufficiently into detail to serve as a foundation for predicting phenomena in the concrete are for the most part only approximately true. But in order to give a genuinely scientific character to the study, it is indispensable that these approximate generalisations, which in themselves would amount only to the lowest kind of empirical laws, should be connected deductively with the laws of nature from which they result – should be resolved into the properties of the causes on which the phenomena depend. In other words, the science of Human Nature may be said to exist in proportion as the approximate truths which compose a practical knowledge of mankind can be exhibited as corollaries from the universal laws of human nature on which they rest, whereby the proper limits of those approximate truths would be shown, and we should be enabled to deduce others for any new state of circumstances, in anticipation of specific experience.

The proposition now stated is the text on which the two succeeding chapers will furnish the comment.

* Book III, Chap. xxiv, § 7.

CHAPTER FOUR

Of the Laws of Mind

1. *What is meant by laws of mind*

What the Mind is, as well as what Matter is, or any other question respecting Things in themselves, as distinguished from their sensible manifestations, it would be foreign to the purposes of this treatise to consider. Here, as throughout our inquiry, we shall keep clear of all speculations respecting the mind's own nature, and shall understand by the laws of mind those of mental phenomena – of the various feelings or states of consciousness of sentient beings. These, according to the classification we have uniformly followed, consist of Thoughts, Emotions, Volitions, and Sensations; the last being as truly states of Mind as the three former. It is usual, indeed, to speak of sensations as states of body, not of mind. But this is the common confusion of giving one and the same name to a phenomenon and to the proximate cause or conditions of the phenomenon. The immediate antecedent of a sensation is a state of body, but the sensation itself is a state of mind. If the word mind means anything, it means that which feels. Whatever opinion we hold respecting the fundamental identity or diversity of matter and mind, in any case the distinction between mental and physical facts, between the internal and the eternal world, will always remain as a matter of classification; and in that classification, sensations, like all other feelings, must be ranked as mental phenomena. The mechanism of their production, both in the body itself and in what is called outward nature, is all that can with any propriety be classed as physical.

The phenomena of mind, then, are the various feelings of our nature, both those improperly called physical and those peculiarly designated as mental; and by the laws of mind I mean the laws according to which those feelings generate one another.

2. Is there a science of psychology?

All states of mind are immediately caused either by other states of mind or by states of body. When a state of mind is produced by a state of mind, I call the law concerned in the case a law of Mind. When a state of mind is produced directly by a state of body, the law is a law of Body, and belongs to physical science.

With regard to those states of mind which are called sensations, all are agreed that these have for their immediate antecedents states of body. Every sensation has for its proximate cause some affection of the portion of our frame called the nervous system, whether this affection originate in the action of some external object, or in some pathological condition of the nervous organisation itself. The laws of this portion of our nature – the varieties of our sensations and the physical conditions on which they proximately depend – manifestly belong to the province of Physiology.

Whether the remainder of our mental states are similarly dependent on physical conditions, is one of the *vexatae questiones* in the science of human nature. It is still disputed whether our thoughts, emotions, and volitions are generated through the intervention of material mechanism; whether we have organs of thought and of emotion in the same sense in which we have organs of sensation. Many eminent physiologists hold the affirmative. These contend that a thought (for example) is as much the result of nervous agency as a sensation; that some particular state of our nervous system, in particular of that central portion of it called the brain, invariably precedes, and is presupposed by, every state of our consciousness. According to this theory, one state of mind is never really produced by another; all are produced by states of body. When one thought seems to call up another by association, it is not really a thought which recalls a thought; the association did not exist between the two thoughts, but between the two states of the brain or nerves which preceded the thoughts: one of those states recalls the other, each being attended, in its passage, by the particular state of consciousness which is consequent on it. On this theory the uniformities of succession among states of mind would be mere derivative uniformities, resulting from the laws of succession of the bodily states which cause them. There would be no original mental laws, no Laws of Mind in the sense in which I use the term, at all; and mental science would be a mere branch, though the highest and most recondite branch, of the science of Physiology. M. Comte, accordingly, claims the scientific cognisance of moral and intellectual phenomena exclusively for physiologists; and not only denies to Psychology, or Mental Philosophy properly so called, the character of a science, but places it, in the chimerical nature of its objects and pretensions, almost on a par with astrology.

But, after all has been said which can be said, it remains incontestable that there exist uniformities of succession among states of mind, and that these can be ascertained by observation and experiment. Further, that every mental state has a nervous state for its immediate antecedent and proximate cause, though extremely probable, cannot hitherto be said to be proved, in the conclusive manner in which this can be proved of sensations; and even were it certain, yet every one must admit that we are wholly ignorant of the characteristics of these nervous states; we know not, and at present have no means of knowing, in what respect one of them differs from another; and our only mode of studying their successions or co-existences must be by observing the successions and co-existences of the mental states of which they are supposed to be the generators or causes. The successions, therefore, which obtain among mental phenomena do not admit of being deduced from the physiological laws of our nervous organisation; and all real knowledge of them must continue, for a long time at least, if not always, to be sought in the direct study, by observation and experiment, of the mental successions themselves. Since, therefore, the order of our mental phenomena must be studied in those phenomena, and not inferred from the laws of any phenomena more general, there is a distinct and separate Science of Mind.

The relations, indeed, of that science to the science of physiology must never be overlooked or undervalued. It must by no means be forgotten that the laws of mind may be derivative laws resulting from laws of animal life, and that their truth therefore may ultimately depend on physical conditions; and the influence of physiological states or physiological changes in altering or counteracting the mental successions is one of the most important departments of psychological study. But, on the other hand, to reject the resource of psychological analysis, and construct the theory of the mind solely on such data as physiology at present affords, seems to me as great an error in principle, and an even more serious one in practice. Imperfect as is the science of mind, I do not scruple to affirm that it is in a considerably more advanced state than the portion of physiology which corresponds to it; and to discard the former for the latter appears to me an infringement of the true canons of inductive philosophy, which must produce, and which does produce, erroneous conclusions in some very important departments of the science of human nature.

3. *The principal investigations of psychology characterised*

The subject, then, of Psychology is the uniformities of succession, the laws, whether ultimate or derivative, according to which one mental state succeeds another – is caused by, or at least is caused to follow, another. Of these laws, some are general, others more special. The following are examples of the most general laws.

First, whenever any state of consciousness has once been excited in us, no matter by what cause, an inferior degree of the same state of consciousness, a state of consciousness resembling the former, but inferior in intensity, is capable of being reproduced in us, without the presence of any such cause as excited it at first. Thus, if we have once seen or touched an object, we can afterwards think of the object though it be absent from our sight or from our touch. If we have been joyful or grieved at some event, we can think of or remember our past joy or grief, though no new event of a happy or painful nature has taken place. When a poet has put together a mental picture of an imaginary object, a Castle of Indolence, a Una, or a Hamlet, he can afterwards think of the ideal object he has created without any fresh act of intellectual combination. This law is expressed by saying, in the language of Hume, that every mental *impression* has its *idea*.

Secondly, these ideas, or secondary mental states, are excited by our impressions, or by other ideas, according to certain laws which are called Laws of Association. Of these laws the first is, that similar ideas tend to excite one another. The second is, that when two impressions have been frequently experienced (or even thought of), either simultaneously or in immediate succession, then whenever one of these impressions, or the idea of it, recurs, it tends to excite the idea of the other. The third law is, that greater intensity in either or both of the impressions is equivalent, in rendering them excitable by one another, to a greater frequency of conjunction. These are the laws of ideas, on which I shall not enlarge in this place, but refer the reader to works professedly psychological, in particular to Mr James Mill's *Analysis of the Phenomena of the Human Mind*, where the principal laws of association, along with many of their applications, are copiously exemplified, and with masterly hand.*

These simple or elementary Laws of Mind have been ascertained by the ordinary methods of experimental inquiry; nor could they have been ascertained in any other manner. But a certain number of elementary laws having thus been obtained, it is a fair subject of scientific inquiry how far those laws can be made to go in explaining the actual phenomena. It is obvious that complex laws of thought and feeling not only may, but must be generated from these simple laws. And it is to be remarked that the case is not always one of Composition of Causes: the effect of concurring causes is not always precisely the sum of the effects of those causes when separate, nor even always an effect of the same kind with them. Reverting to the distinction which occupies so prominent a place in the theory of induction, the laws of the phenomena of mind are sometimes analogous to mechanical, but sometimes also to chemical laws. When many impressions or ideas are operating in the mind together, there sometimes takes place a process of a similar kind to chemical combination. When impressions have been so often experienced in conjunction that each of them calls up readily and instantaneously the ideas of the whole group, those ideas sometimes melt and coalesce into one another, and appear not several ideas, but one, in the same manner as, when the seven prismatic colours are presented to the eye in rapid succession the sensation produced is that of white.

* When this chapter was written, Professor Bain had not yet published even the first part (*The Senses and the Intellect*) of his profound *Treatise on the Mind*. In this the laws of association have been more comprehensively stated and more largely exemplified than by any previous writer; and the work, having been completed by the publication of *The Emotions and the Will*, may now be referred to as incomparably the most complete analytical exposition of the mental phenomena, on the basis of a legitimate induction, which has yet been produced. More recently still, Mr Bain has joined with me in appending to a new edition of the *Analysis* notes intended to bring up the analytic science of Mind to its latest improvements.

Many striking applications of the laws of association to the explanation of complex mental phenomena are also to be found in Mr Herbert Spencer's *Principles of Psychology*.

But as in this last case it is correct to say that the seven colours when they rapidly follow one another *generate* white, but not that they actually *are* white; so it appears to me that the Complex Idea, formed by the blending together of several simpler ones, should, when it really appears simple, (that is, when the separate elements are not consciously distinguishable in it,) be said to *result from,* or *be generated by*, the simple ideas, not to *consist* of them. Our idea of an orange really *consists* of the simple ideas of a certain colour, a certain form, a certain taste and smell, etc., because we can, by interrogating our consciousness, perceive all these elements in the idea. But we cannot perceive, in so apparently simple a feeling as our perception of the shape of an object by the eye, all that multitude of ideas derived from other senses, without which it is well ascertained that no such visual perception would ever have had existence; nor, in our idea of Extension, can we discover those elementary ideas of resistance derived from our muscular frame in which it had been conclusively shown that the idea originates. These, therefore, are cases of mental chemistry, in which it is proper to say that the simple ideas generate, rather than that they compose, the complex ones.

With respect to all the other constituents of the mind, its beliefs, its abstruser conceptions, its sentiments, emotions, and volitions, there are some (among whom are Hartley and the author of the *Analysis*) who think that the whole of these are generated from simple ideas of sensation by a chemistry similar to that which we have just exemplified. These philosophers have made out a great part of their case, but I am not satisfied that they have established the whole of it. They have shown that there is such a thing as mental chemistry; that the heterogeneous nature of a feeling A, considered in relation to B and C, is no conclusive argument against its being generated from B and C. Having proved this, they proceed to show that where A is found B and C were or may have been present; and why, therefore, they ask, should not A have been generated from B and C? But even if this evidence were carried to the highest degree of completeness which it admits of; if it were shown (which hitherto it has not, in all cases, been) that certain groups of associated ideas not only might have been, but actually were present whenever the more recondite mental feeling was experienced, this would amount only to the Method of Agreement, and could not prove causation until confirmed by the more conclusive evidence of the Method of

Difference. If the question be whether Belief is a mere case of close association of ideas, it would be necessary to examine experimentally if it be true that any ideas whatever, provided they are associated with the required degree of closeness, give rise to belief. If the inquiry be into the origin of moral feelings, the feeling, for example, of moral reprobation, it is necessary to compare all the varieties of actions or states of mind which are ever morally disapproved, and see whether in all these cases it can be shown, or reasonably surmised, that the action or state of mind had become connected by association, in the disapproving mind, with some particular class of hateful or disgusting ideas; and the method employed is, thus far, that of Agreement. But this is not enough. Supposing this proved, we must try further by the Method of Difference whether this particular kind of hateful or disgusting ideas, when it becomes associated with an action previously indifferent, will render that action a subject of moral disapproval. If this question can be answered in the affirmative, it is shown to be a law of the human mind that an association of that particular description is the generating cause of moral reprobation. That all this is the case has been rendered extremely probable, but the experiments have not been tried with the degree of precision necessary for a complete and absolutely conclusive induction.*

It is further to be remembered, that even if all which this theory of mental phenomena contends for could be proved, we should not be the more enabled to resolve the laws of the more complex feelings into those of the simpler ones. The generation of one class of mental phenomena from another, whenever it can be made out, is a highly interesting fact in psychological chemistry; but it no more supersedes the necessity of an experimental study of the generated phenomenon, than a knowledge of the properties of oxygen and sulphur enables us to deduce those of sulphuric acid without specific observation and experiment. Whatever, therefore, may be the final issue of the attempt to account for the origin of our judgments, our desires, or our volitions, from simpler mental phenomena, it is not the less

* In the case of the moral sentiments, the place of direct experiment is to a considerable extent supplied by historical experience, and we are able to trace with a tolerable approach to certainty the particular associations by which those sentiments are engendered. This has been attempted, so far as respects the sentiment of justice, in a little work by the present author, entitled *Utilitarianism*.

imperative to ascertain the sequences of the complex phenomena themselves by special study in conformity to the canons of Induction. Thus, in respect to Belief, psychologists will always have to inquire what beliefs we have by direct consciousness, and according to what laws one belief produces another; what are the laws in virtue of which one thing is recognised by the mind, either rightly or erroneously, as evidence of another thing. In regard to Desire, they will have to examine what objects we desire naturally, and by what causes we are made to desire things originally indifferent, or even disagreeable to us; and so forth. It may be remarked, that the general laws of association prevail among these more intricate states of mind, in the same manner as among the simpler ones. A desire, an emotion, an idea of the higher order of abstraction, even our judgments and volitions when they have become habitual, are called up by association, according to precisely the same laws as our simple ideas.

4. *Relation of mental facts to physical conditions*

In the course of these inquiries it will be natural and necessary to examine how far the production of one state of mind by another is influenced by any assignable state of body. The commonest observation shows that different minds are susceptible in very different degrees to the action of the same psychological causes. The idea, for example, of a given desirable object will excite in different minds very different degrees of intensity of desire. The same subject of meditation presented to different minds, will excite in them very unequal degrees of intellectual action. These differences of mental susceptibility in different individuals may be, first, original and ultimate facts, or, secondly, they may be consequences of the previous mental history of those individuals, or, thirdly and lastly, they may depend on varieties of physical organisation. That the previous mental history of the individuals must have some share in producing or in modifying the whole of their mental character is an inevitable consequence of the laws of mind; but that differences of bodily structure also co-operate is the opinion of all physiologists, confirmed by common experience. It is to be regretted that hitherto this experience, being accepted in the gross without due analysis, has been made the groundwork of empirical generalisations most detrimental to the progress of real knowledge.

It is certain that the natural differences which really exist in the mental predispositions or susceptibilities of different persons, are often not unconnected with diversities in their organic constitution. But it does not therefore follow that these organic differences must in all cases influence the mental phenomena directly and immediately. They often affect them through the medium of their psychological causes. For example, the idea of some particular pleasure may excite in different persons, even independently of habit or education, very different strengths of desire, and this may be the effect of their different degrees or kinds of nervous susceptibility; but these organic differences, we must remember, will render the pleasurable sensation itself more intense in one of these persons than in the other; so that the idea of the pleasure will also be an intenser feeling, and will, by the operation of mere mental laws, excite an intenser desire, without its being necessary to suppose that the desire itself is directly influenced by the physical peculiarity. As in this, so in many cases, such differences in the kind or in the intensity of the physical sensations as must necessarily result from differences of bodily organisation will of themselves account for many differences, not only in the degree, but even in the kind, of the other mental phenomena. So true is this, that even different *qualities* of mind, different types of mental character, will naturally be produced by mere differences of intensity in the sensations generally: as is well pointed out in the able essay on Dr Priestley by Mr Martineau, mentioned in a former chapter:

> The sensations which form the elements of all knowledge are received either simultaneously or successively; when several are received simultaneously, as the smell, the taste, the colour, the form, etc., of a fruit, their association together constitutes our idea of an *object*; when received successively, their association makes up the idea of an *event*. Anything, then, which favours the associations of synchronous ideas will tend to produce a knowledge of objects, a perception of qualities; while anything which favours association in the successive order will tend to produce a knowledge of events, of the order of occurrences, and of the connection of cause and effect: in other words, in the one case a perceptive mind, with a discriminate feeling of the pleasurable and painful properties of things, a sense of the grand and the beautiful will be the result; in the other, a mind attentive to the movements and phenomena, a ratiocinative and philosophic intellect. Now it is an

acknowledged principle that all sensations experienced during the presence of any vivid impression become strongly associated with it and with each other, and does it not follow that the synchronous feelings of a sensitive constitution (*i.e.* the one which has vivid impressions) will be more intimately blended than in a differently formed mind? If this suggestion has any foundation in truth, it leads to an inference not unimportant; that when nature has endowed an individual with great original susceptibility, he will probably be distinguished by fondness for natural history, a relish for the beautiful and great, and moral enthusiasm; where there is but a mediocrity of sensibility, a love of science, of abstract truth, with a deficiency of taste and of fervour, is likely to be the result.

We see from this example that when the general laws of mind are more accurately known, and, above all, more skilfully applied to the detailed explanation of mental peculiarities, they will account for many more of those peculiarities than is ordinarily supposed. Unfortunately the reaction of the last and present generation against the philosophy of the eighteenth century has produced a very general neglect of this great department of analytical inquiry, of which, consequently, the recent progress has been by no means proportional to its early promise. The majority of those who speculate on human nature prefer dogmatically to assume that the mental differences which they perceive, or think they perceive, among human beings are ultimate facts, incapable of being either explained or altered, rather than take the trouble of fitting themselves, by the requisite processes of thought, for referring those mental differences to the outward causes by which they are for the most part produced, and on the removal of which they would cease to exist. The German school of metaphysical speculation, which has not yet lost its temporary predominance in European thought, has had this among many other injurious influences; and at the opposite extreme of the psychological scale, no writer, either of early or of recent date, is chargeable in a higher degree with this aberration from the true scientific spirit than M. Comte.

It is certain that, in human beings at least, differences in education and in outward circumstances are capable of affording an adequate explanation of by far the greatest portion of character, and that the remainder may be in great part accounted for by physical differences in the sensations produced in different individuals by the same external or internal cause. There are, however, some mental facts which do not seem to admit of these modes of explanation. Such, to take the strongest case, are the various instincts of animals, and the portion of human nature which corresponds to those instincts. No mode has been suggested, even by way of hypothesis, in which these can receive any satisfactory, or even plausible, explanation from psychological causes alone; and there is great reason to think that they have as positive, and even as direct and immediate, a connection with physical conditions of the brain and nerves as any of our mere sensations have. A supposition which (it is perhaps not superfluous to add) in no way conflicts with the indisputable fact that these instincts may be modified to any extent, or entirely conquered, in human beings, and to no inconsiderable extent even in some of the domesticated animals, by other mental influences, and by education.

Whether organic causes exercise a direct influence over any other classes of mental phenomena is hitherto as far from being ascertained as is the precise nature of the organic conditions even in the case of instincts. The physiology, however, of the brain and nervous system is in a state of such rapid advance, and is continually bringing forth such new and interesting results, that if there be really a connection between mental peculiarities and any varieties cognisable by our senses in the structure of the cerebral and nervous apparatus, the nature of that connection is now in a fair way of being found out. The latest discoveries in cerebral physiology appear to have proved that any such connection which may exist is of a radically different character from that contended for by Gall and his followers, and that whatever may hereafter be found to be the true theory of the subject, phrenology at least is untenable.

CHAPTER FIVE

Of Ethology, or the Science of the Formation of Character

1. The empirical laws of human nature

The laws of mind, as characterised in the preceding chapter, compose the universal or abstract portion of the philosophy of human nature; and all the truths of common experience, constituting a practical knowledge of mankind, must, to the extent to which they are truths, be results of consequences of these. Such familiar maxims, when collected *à posteriori* from observation of life, occupy among the truths of the science the place of what, in our analysis of Induction, have so often been spoken of under the title of Empirical Laws.

An Empirical Law (it will be remembered) is an uniformity, whether of succession or of co-existence, which holds true in all instances within our limits of observation, but is not of a nature to afford any assurance that it would hold beyond those limits, either because the consequent is not really the effect of the antecedent, but forms part along with it of a chain of effects, flowing from prior causes not yet ascertained, or because there is ground to believe that the sequence (though a case of causation) is resolvable into simpler sequences, and, depending therefore on a concurrence of several natural agencies, is exposed to an unknown multitude of possibilities of counteraction. In other words, an empirical law is a generalisation, of which, not content with finding it true, we are obliged to ask why is it true? knowing that its truth is not absolute, but dependent on some more general conditions, and that it can only be relied on in so far as there is ground of assurance that those conditions are realised.

Now, the observations concerning human affairs collected from common experience are precisely of this nature. Even if they were universally and exactly true within the bounds of experience, which they never are, still they are not the ultimate laws of human action; they are not the principles of human nature, but results of those principles under the circumstance in which mankind have happened to be placed. When the Psalmist 'said in his haste that all men are liars', he enunciated what in some ages and countries is borne out by ample experience; but it is not a law of man's nature to lie, though it is one of the consequences of the laws of the human nature that lying is nearly universal when certain external circumstances exist universally, especially circumstances productive of habitual distrust and fear. When the character of the old is asserted to be cautious, and of the young impetuous, this, again, is but an empirical law; for it is not because of their youth that the young are impetuous, nor because of their age that the old are cautious. It is chiefly, if not wholly, because the old, during their many years of life, have generally had much experience of its various evils, and having suffered or seen others suffer much from incautious exposure to them, have acquired associations favourable to circumspection; while the young, as well from the absence of similar experience as from the greater strength of the inclinations which urge them to enterprise, engage themselves in it more readily. Here, then, is the *explanation* of the empirical law; here are the conditions which ultimately determine whether the law holds good or not. If an old man has not been oftener than most young men in contact with danger and difficulty, he will be equally incautious: if a youth has not stronger inclinations than an old man, he probably will be as little enterprising. The empirical law derives whatever truth it has from the causal laws of which it is a consequence. If we know those laws, we know what are the limits to the derivative law; while, if we have not yet accounted for the empirical law – if it rests only on observation – there is no safety in applying it far beyond the limits of time, place, and circumstance in which the observations were made.

The really scientific truths, then, are not these empirical laws, but the causal laws which explain them. The empirical laws of those phenomena which depend on known causes, and of which a general theory can therefore be constructed, have, whatever may be their value in practice, no other function in science than that of verifying the conclusions of theory. Still more must this be the case when most of the empirical laws amount, even within the limits of observation, only to approximate generalisations.

2. They are merely approximate generalisations. The universal laws are those of the formation of character

This, however, is not, so much as is sometimes supposed, a peculiarity of the sciences called moral. It is only in the simplest branches of science that empirical laws are ever exactly true, and not always in those. Astronomy, for example, is the simplest of all the sciences which explain, in the concrete, the actual course of natural events. The causes or forces on which astronomical phenomena depend are fewer in number than those which determine any other of the great phenomena of nature. Accordingly, as each effect results from the conflict of but few causes, a great degree of regularity and uniformity might be expected to exist among the effects; and such is really the case: they have a fixed order and return in cycles. But propositions which should express with absolute correctness all the successive positions of a planet until the cycle is completed would be of almost unmanageable complexity, and could be obtained from theory alone. The generalisations which can be collected on the subject from direct observation, even such as Kepler's law, are mere approximations: the planets, owing to their perturbations by one another, do not move in exact ellipses. Thus even in astronomy perfect exactness in the mere empirical laws is not be looked for; much less, then, in more complex subjects of inquiry.

The same example shows how little can be inferred against the universality, or even the simplicity of the ultimate laws, from the impossibility of establishing any but approximate empirical laws of the effects. The laws of causation according to which a class of phenomena are produced may be very few and simple, and yet the effects themselves may be so various and complicated that it shall be impossible to trace any regularity whatever completely through them. For the phenomena in question may be of an eminently modifiable character, insomuch that innumerable circumstances are capable of influencing the effect, although they may all do it according to a very small number of laws. Suppose that all which passes in the mind of man is determined by a few simple laws: still, if those laws be such that there is not one of the facts surrounding a human being, or of the events which happen to him, that does not influence in some mode or degree his subsequent mental history, and if the circumstances of different human beings are extremely different, it will be no wonder if very few propositions can be made respecting the details of their conduct or feelings which will be true of all mankind.

Now, without deciding whether the ultimate laws of our mental nature are few or many, it is at least certain that they are of the above description. It is certain that our mental states, and our mental capacities and susceptibilities, are modified, either for a time or permanently, by everything which happens to us in life. Considering, therefore, how much these modifying causes differ in the case of any two individuals, it would be unreasonable to expect that the empirical laws of the human mind, the generalisations which can be made respecting the feelings or actions of mankind without reference to the causes that determine them, should be anything but approximate generalisations. They are the common wisdom of common life, and as such are invaluable; especially as they are mostly to be applied to cases not very dissimilar to those from which they were collected. But when maxims of this sort, collected from Englishmen, come to be applied to Frenchmen, or when those collected from the present day are applied to past or future generations, they are apt to be very much at fault. Unless we have resolved the empirical law into the law of the causes on which it depends, and ascertained that those causes extend to the case which we have in view, there can be no reliance placed in our inferences. For every individual is surrounded by circumstances different from those of every other individual; every nation or generation of mankind from every other nation or generation; and none of these differences are without their influence in forming a different type of character. There is, indeed, also a certain general resemblance; but peculiarities of circumstances are continually constituting exceptions even to the propositions which are true in the great majority of cases.

Although, however, there is scarcely any mode of feeling or conduct which is, in the absolute sense, common to all mankind; and though the generalisations which assert that any given variety of conduct or feeling will be found universally, (however nearly they may approximate to truth within given limits of observation,) will be considered as scientific propositions by no one who is at all familiar with scientific investigation; yet all modes of feeling and conduct met with among mankind have causes which produce them; and in the propositions which assign those causes will be found the explanation of the empirical laws, and the limiting principle of our reliance on them. Human beings do not all feel and act alike in the same circumstances; but it is possible to determine what makes one person, in a given position, feel or act in one way, another in another; how any given mode of feeling and conduct, compatible with the general laws (physical and mental) of human nature, has been, or may be, formed. In other words, mankind have not one universal character, but there exist universal laws of the Formation of Character. And since it is by these laws, combined with the facts of each particular case, that the whole of the phenomena of human action and feeling are produced, it is on these that every rational attempt to construct the science of human nature in the concrete and for practical purposes must proceed.

3. *The laws of the formation of character cannot be ascertained by observation and experiment*

The laws, then, of the formation of character being the principal object of scientific inquiry into human nature, it remains to determine the method of investigation best fitted for ascertaining them. And the logical principles according to which this question is to be decided must be those which preside over every other attempt to investigate the laws of very complex phenomena. For it is evident that both the character of any human being, and the aggregate of the circumstances by which that character has been formed, are facts of a high order of complexity. Now to such cases we have seen that the Deductive Method, setting out from general laws, and verifying their consequences by specific experience, is alone applicable. The grounds of this great logical doctrine have formerly been stated, and its truth will derive additional support from a brief examination of the specialities of the present case.

There are only two modes in which laws of nature can be ascertained deductively and experimentally, including under the denomination of experimental inquiry, observation as well as artificial experiment. Are the laws of the formation of character susceptible of a satisfactory investigation by the method of experimentation? Evidently not; because, even if we suppose unlimited power of varying the experiment, (which is abstractedly possible, though no one but an Oriental despot has that power, or, if he had, would probably be disposed to exercise it,) a still more essential condition is wanting – the power of performing any of the experiments with scientific accuracy.

The instances requisite for the prosecution of a directly experimental inquiry into the formation of character would be a number of human beings to bring up and educate from infancy to mature age; and to perform any one of these experiments with scientific propriety, it would be necessary to know and record every sensation or impression received by the young pupil from a period long before it could speak, including its own notions respecting the sources of all those sensations and impressions. It is not only impossible to do this completely, but even to do so much of it as should constitute a tolerable approximation. One apparently trivial circumstance which eluded our vigilance might let in a train of impressions and associations sufficient to vitiate the experiment as an authentic exhibition of the effects flowing from given causes. No one who has sufficiently reflected on education is ignorant of this truth: and whoever has not will find it most instructively illustrated in the writing of Rousseau and Helvetius on that great subject.

Under this impossibility of studying the laws of the formation of character by experiments purposely contrived to elucidate them there remains the resource of simple observation. But if it be impossible to ascertain the influencing circumstances with any approach to completeness even when we have the shaping of them ourselves, much more impossible is it when the cases are further removed from our observation, and altogether out of our control. Consider the difficulty of the very first step – of ascertaining what actually is the character of the individual in each particular case that we examine. There is hardly any person living, concerning some essential part of whose character there are not differences of opinion even among his intimate acquaintances; and a single action, or conduct continued only for a short time, goes a very little way towards ascertaining it. We can only make our observations in a rough way and *en masse*, not attempting to ascertain completely in any given instance what character has been formed, and still less by what causes; but only observing in what state of previous circumstances it is found that certain marked mental qualities or deficiencies *oftenest* exist. These conclusions, besides that they are mere approximate generalisations, deserve no reliance, even as such, unless the instances are sufficiently numerous to eliminate not only chance, but every assignable circumstance in which a number of the cases examined may happen to have resembled one another. So numerous and various, too, are the circumstances which form individual character, that the consequence of any particular combination is hardly ever some definite and strongly marked character, always found where that combination exists, and not otherwise. What is obtained, even after the most extensive and accurate observations, is merely a comparative result; as, for example, that in a given number of Frenchmen, taken indiscriminately, there will be found more persons of a particular mental tendency, and fewer of the contrary tendency, than among an equal number of Italians or English, similarly taken; or thus: of a hundred Frenchmen and an equal number of Englishmen, fairly selected, and arranged according to the degree in which they possess a particular mental characteristic, each number 1, 2, 3, of the one series will be found to possess more of that characteristic than the corresponding number of the other. Since, therefore, the comparison is not one of kinds, but of ratios and degrees; and since in proportion as the differences are slight, it requires a greater number of instances to eliminate chance; it cannot often happen to any one to know a sufficient number of cases with the accuracy requisite for making the sort of comparison last mentioned; less than which, however, would not constitute a real induction. Accordingly there is hardly one current opinion respecting the characters of nations, classes, or descriptions of persons, which is universally acknowledged as indisputable.*

---

* The most favourable cases for making such approximate generalisations are what may be termed collective instances, where we are fortunately enabled to see the whole class respecting which we are inquiring in action at once, and, from the qualities displayed by the collective body, are able to judge what must be the qualities of the majority of the individuals composing it. Thus the character of a nation is shown in its acts as a nation; not so much in the acts of its government, for those are much influenced by other causes; but in the current popular maxims, and other marks of the general direction of public opinion; in the character of the persons or writings that are held in permanent esteem or admiration; in laws and institutions, so far as they are the work of the nation itself, or are acknowledged and supported by it; and so forth. But even here there is a large margin of doubt and uncertainty. These things are liable to be influenced by many circumstances: they are partly determined by the distinctive

And finally, if we could even obtain by way of experiment a much more satisfactory assurance of these generalisations than is really possible, they would still be only empirical laws. They would show, indeed, that there was some connection between the type of character formed and the circumstances existing in the case, but not what the precise connection was, nor to which of the peculiarities of those circumstances the effect was really owing. They could only, therefore, be received as results of causation, requiring to be resolved into the general laws of the causes: until the determination of which, we could not judge within what limits the derivative laws might serve as presumptions in cases yet unknown, or even be depended on as permanent in the very cases from which they were collected. The French people had, or were supposed to have, a certain national character; but they drive out their royal family and aristocracy, alter their institutions, pass through a series of extraordinary events for the greater part of a century, and at the end of that time their character is found to have undergone important changes. A long list of mental and moral differences are observed, or supposed to exist, between men and women; but at some future, and, it may be hoped, not distant period, equal freedom and an equally independent social position come to be possessed by both, and their differences of character are either removed or totally altered.

But if the differences which we think we observe between French and English, or between men and women, can be connected with more general laws; if they be such as might be expected to be produced by the differences of government, former customs, and physical peculiarities in the two nations, and by the diversities of education, occupations, personal independence, and social privileges, and whatever original differences there may be in bodily strength and nervous sensibility between the two sexes; then, indeed, the coincidence of the two kinds of evidence justifies us in believing that we have both reasoned rightly and observed rightly. Our

---

qualities of that nation or body of persons but partly also by external causes which would influence any other body of persons, in the same manner. In order, therefore, to make the experiment really complete, we ought to be able to try it without variation upon other nations: to try how Englishmen would act or feel if placed in the same circumstances in which we have supposed Frenchmen to be placed; to apply, in short, the Method of Difference as well as that of Agreement. Now these experiments we cannot try, nor even approximate to.

observation, though not sufficient as proof, is ample as verification. And having ascertained not only the empirical laws, but the causes of the peculiarities, we need be under no difficulty in judging how far they may be expected to be permanent, or by what circumstances they would be modified or destroyed.

4. *They must be studied deductively*

Since, then, it is impossible to obtain really accurate propositions respecting the formation of character from observation and experiment alone, we are driven perforce to that which, even if it had not been the indispensable, would have been the most perfect mode of investigation, and which it is one of the principal aims of philosophy to extend; namely, that which tries its experiments not on the complex facts, but on the simple ones of which they are compounded, and after ascertaining the laws of the causes, the composition of which gives rise to the complex phenomena, then considers whether these will not explain and account for the approximate generalis-ations which have been framed empirically respecting the sequences of those complex phenomena. The laws of the formation of character are, in short, derivative laws, resulting from the general laws of mind, and are to be obtained by deducing them from those general laws by supposing any given set of circumstances, and then considering what, according to the laws of mind, will be the influence of those circumstances on the formation of character.

A science is thus formed, to which I would propose to give the name of Ethology, or the Science of Character, from *êthos*, a word more nearly corresponding to the term 'character', as I here use it, than any other word in the same language. The name is perhaps etymologically applicable to the entire science of our mental and moral nature; but if, as is usual and convenient, we employ the name Psychology for the science of the elementary laws of mind, Ethology will serve for the ulterior science which determines the kind of character produced in conformity to those general laws, by any set of circumstances, physical and moral. According to this definition, Ethology is the science which corresponds to the act of education, in the widest sense of the term, including the formation of national or collective character as well as individual. It would indeed be vain to expect (however completely the laws of the formation of character might be ascertained) that we could know so accurately the circumstances of any given case as to be able positively to predict the character that would be produced in that case. But we must remember that a degree of knowledge far short of the power of actual prediction is often of much practical value. There may be great power of influencing phenomena, with a very imperfect knowledge of the causes by which they are in any given instance determined. It is enough that we know that certain means have a *tendency* to produce a given effect, and that others have a tendency to frustrate it. When the circumstances of an individual or of a nation are in any considerable degree under our control, we may, by our knowledge of tendencies, be enabled to shape those circumstances in a manner much more favourable to the ends we desire than the shape which they would of themselves assume. This is the limit of our power, but within this limit the power is a most important one.

This science of Ethology may be called the Exact Science of Human Nature; for its truths are not, like the empirical laws which depend on them, approximate generalisations, but real laws. It is, however, (as in all cases of complex phenomena,) necessary to the exactness of the propositions that they should be hypothetical only, and affirm tendencies, not facts. They must not assert that something will always or certainly happen, but only that such and such will be the effect of a given cause, so far as it operates uncounteracted. It is a scientific proposition that bodily strength tends to make men courageous; not that it always makes them so: that an interest on one side of a question tends to bias the judgment; not that it invariably does so: that experience tends to give wisdom; not that such is always its effect. These propositions, being assertive only of tendencies, are not the less universally true because the tendencies may be frustrated.

5. *The principles of ethology are the* axiomata media *of mental science*

While, on the other hand, Psychology is altogether, or principally, a science of observation and experiment, Ethology, as I have conceived it, is, as I have already remarked, altogether deductive. The one ascertains the simple laws of Mind in general, the other traces their operation in complex combinations of circumstances. Ethology stands to Psychology in a relation very similar to that in which the various branches of natural philosophy stand to mechanics. The principles of Ethology are properly the middle principles, the *axiomata media* (as Bacon would have said) of the science of mind: as distinguished, on the one hand, from the empirical laws resulting from simple observation, and on the other from the highest generalisations.

And this seems a suitable place for a logical remark, which, though of general application, is of peculiar importance in reference to the present subject. Bacon has judiciously observed that the *axiomata media* of every science principally constitute its value. The lowest generalisations, until explained by and resolved into the middle principles of which they are the consequences, have only the imperfect accuracy of empirical laws; while the most general laws are *too* general, and include too few circumstances to give sufficient indication of what happens in individual cases where the circumstances are almost always immensely numerous. In the importance, therefore, which Bacon assigns in every science to the middle principles, it is impossible not to agree with him. But I conceive him to have been radically wrong in his doctrine respecting the mode in which these *axiomata media* should be arrived at; though there is no one proposition laid down in his works for which he has been more extravagantly eulogised. He enunciates as an universal rule that induction should proceed from the lowest to the middle principles, and from those to the highest, never reversing that order, and consequently, leaving no room for the discovery of new principles by way of deduction at all. It is not to be conceived that a man of his sagacity could have fallen into this mistake if there had existed in his time, among the sciences which treat of successive phenomena, one single instance of a deductive science, such as mechanics, astronomy, optics, acoustics, etc., now are. In those sciences it is evident that the higher and middle principles are by no means derived from the lowest, but the reverse. In some of them the very highest generalisations were those earliest ascertained with any scientific exactness; as, for example, (in mechanics,) the laws of motion. Those general laws had not indeed at first the acknowledged universality which they acquired after having been successfully employed to explain many classes of phenomena to which they were not originally seen to be applicable; as when the laws of motion were employed, in conjunction with other laws, to explain deductively the celestial phenomena. Still the fact remains that the propositions which were afterwards recognised as the most general truths of the science were, of all its accurate generalisations, those earliest arrived at. Bacon's greatest merit cannot therefore consist, as we are so often told that it did, in exploding the vicious method pursued by the ancients of flying to the highest generalisations first, and deducing the middle principles from them; since this is neither a vicious nor an exploded, but the universally accredited method of modern science, and that to which it owes its greatest triumphs. The error of ancient speculation did not consist in making the largest generalisation first, but in making them without the aid or warrant of rigorous inductive methods, and applying them deductively without the needful use of that important part of the Deductive Method termed Verification.

The order in which truths of the various degrees of generality should be ascertained cannot, I apprehend, be prescribed by any unbending rule. I know of no maxim which can be laid down on the subject, but to obtain those first in respect to which the conditions of a real induction can be first and most completely realised. Now, wherever our means of investigation can reach causes, without stopping at the empirical laws of the effects, the simplest cases being those in which fewest causes are simultaneously concerned, will be most amenable to the inductive process; and these are the cases which elicit laws of the greatest comprehensiveness. In every science, therefore, which has reached the stage at which it becomes a science of causes, it will be usual, as well as desirable, first to obtain the highest generalisations, and then deduce the more special ones from them. Nor can I discover any foundation for the Baconian maxim, so much extolled by subsequent writers, except this: That before we attempt to explain deductively from more general laws any new class of phenomena, it is desirable to have gone as far as is practicable in ascertaining the empirical laws of those phenomena, so as to compare the results of deduction not with one individual instance after another, but with general propositions expressive of the points of agreement which have been found among many instances. For if Newton had been obliged to verify the theory of gravitation, not by deducing from it Kepler's laws, but by deducing all the observed planetary positions which had served Kepler to establish those laws, the Newtonian theory would probably never have emerged from the state of an hypothesis.*

The applicability of these remarks to the special case under consideration cannot admit of question. The science of the formation of character is a science of causes. The subject is one to which those among the canons of induction, by which laws of causation are ascertained, can be rigorously applied. It is, therefore, both natural and advisable to ascertain the simplest, which are necessarily the most general, laws of causation first, and to deduce the middle principles from them. In other words, Ethology, the deductive science, is a system of corollaries from Psychology, the experimental science.

6. Ethology characterised

Of these, the earlier alone has been, as yet, really conceived or studied as a science; the other, Ethology, is still to be created. But its creation has at length become practicable. The empirical laws, destined to verify its deductions, have been formed in abundance by every successive age of humanity, and the premises for the deductions are now sufficiently complete. Excepting the degree of uncertainty which still exists as to the extent of the natural differences of individual minds, and the physical circumstances on which these may be dependent, (considerations which are of secondary importance when we are considering mankind in the average, or *en masse*,) I believe most competent judges will agree that the general laws of the different constituent elements of human nature are even

---

* 'To which,' says Dr Whewell, 'we may add, that it is certain from the history of the subject, that in that case the hypothesis would never have been framed at all.'

Dr Whewell (*Philosophy of Discovery*, pp. 277-82) defends Bacon's rule against the preceding strictures. But his defence consists only in asserting and exemplifying a proposition which I had myself stated, viz. that though the largest generalisations may be the earliest made, they are not at first seen in their entire generality, but acquire it by degrees, as they are found to explain one class after another of phenomena. The laws of motion, for example, were not known to extend to the celestial regions until the motions of the celestial bodies had been deduced from them. This, however, does not in any way affect the fact that the middle principles of astronomy, the central force, for example, and the law of the inverse square, could not have been discovered if the laws of motion, which are so much more universal, had not been known first. On Bacon's system of step-by-step generalisation, it would be impossible in any science to ascend higher than the empirical laws; a remark which Dr Whewell's own Inductive Tables, referred to by him in support of his argument, amply bear out.

now sufficiently understood to render it possible for a competent thinker to deduce from those laws, with a considerable approach to certainty, the particular type of character which would be formed in mankind generally by any assumed set of circumstances. A science of Ethology, founded on the laws of Psychology, is therefore possible, though little has yet been done, and that little not at all systematically, towards forming it. The progress of this important but most imperfect science will depend on a double process: first, that of deducing theoretically the ethological consequences of particular circumstances of position, and comparing them with the recognised results of common experience; and secondly, the reverse operation – increased study of the various types of human nature that are to be found in the world, conducted by persons not only capable of analysing and recording the circumstances in which these types severally prevail, but also sufficiently acquainted with psychological laws to be able to explain and account for the characteristics of the type by the peculiarities of the circumstances, the residuum alone, when there proves to be any, being set down to the account of congenital predisposition.

For the experimental or *à posteriori* part of this process, the materials are continually accumulating by the observation of mankind. So far as thought is concerned, the great problem of Ethology is to deduce the requisite middle principles from the general laws of Psychology. The subject to be studied is, the origin and sources of all those qualities in human beings which are interesting to us, either as facts to be produced, to be avoided, or merely to be understood; and the object is to determine, from the general laws of mind, combined with the general position of our species in the universe, what actual or possible combinations of circumstances are capable of promoting or of preventing the production of those qualities. A science which possesses middle principles of this kind, arranged in the order, not of causes, but of the effects which it is desirable to produce or to prevent, is duly prepared to be the foundation of the corresponding Art. And when Ethology shall be thus prepared, practical education will be the mere transformation of those principles into a parallel system of precepts, and the adaptation of these to the sum total of the individual circumstances which exist in each particular case.

It is hardly necessary again to repeat, that, as in every other deductive science, verification *à posteriori* must proceed *pari passu* with deduction *à priori*. The inference given by theory as to the type of character which would be formed by any given circumstances must be tested by specific experience of those circumstances whenever obtainable; and the conclusions of the science as a whole must undergo a perpetual verification and correction from the general remarks afforded by common experience respecting human nature in our own age, and by history respecting times gone by. The conclusions of theory cannot be trusted, unless confirmed by observation; nor those of observation, unless they can be affiliated to theory, by deducing them from the laws of human nature, and from a close analysis of the circumstances of the particular situation. It is the accordance of these two kinds of evidence separately taken – the consilience of *à priori* reasoning and specific experience – which forms the only sufficient ground for the principles of any science so 'immersed in matter', dealing with such complex and concrete phenomena, as Ethology.

CHAPTER SIX

General Considerations on the Social Science

1. Are social phenomena a subject of science?

Next after the science of individual man comes the science of man in society; of the actions of collective masses of mankind, and the various phenomena which constitute social life.

If the formation of individual character is already a complex subject of study, this subject must be, in appearance at least, still more complex; because the number of concurrent causes, all exercising more or less influence on the total effect, is greater, in the proportion in which a nation, or the species at large, exposes a larger surface to the operation of agents, psychological and physical, than any single individual. If it was necessary to prove, in opposition to an existing prejudice, that the simpler of the two is capable of being a subject of science; the prejudice is likely to be yet stronger against the possibility of giving a scientific character to the study of Politics, and of the phenomena of Society. It is, accordingly, but of yesterday that the conception of a political or social science has existed anywhere but in the mind of here and there an insulated thinker, generally very ill prepared for its realisation: though the subject itself has of all others engaged the most general attention, and been a theme of interested and earnest discussions, almost from the beginning of recorded time.

The condition indeed of politics, as a branch of knowledge, was until very lately, and has scarcely even yet ceased to be, that which Bacon animadverted on, as the natural state of the sciences while their cultivation is abandoned to practitioners; not being carried on as a branch of speculative inquiry, but only with a view to the exigencies of daily practice, and the *fructifera experimenta*, therefore, being aimed at, almost to the exclusion of the *lucifera*. Such was medical investigation before physiology and natural history began to be cultivated as branches of general knowledge. The only questions examined were, what diet is wholesome, or what medicine will cure some given disease, without any previous systematic inquiry into the laws of nutrition, and of the healthy and morbid action of the different organs, on which laws the effect of any diet or medicine must evidently depend. And in politics, the questions which engaged general attention were similar: – Is such an enactment, or such a form of government, beneficial or the reverse – either universally, or to some particular community? without any previous inquiry into the general conditions by which the operation of legislative measures, or the effects produced by forms of government, are determined. Students in politics thus attempted to study the pathology and therapeutics of the social body before they had laid the necessary foundation in its physiology; to cure disease without understanding the laws of health. And the result was such as it must always be when persons, even of ability, attempt to deal with the complex questions of a science before its simpler and more elementary truths have been established.

No wonder that when the phenomena of society have so rarely been contemplated in the point of view characteristic of science, the philosophy of society should have made little progress; should contain few general propositions sufficiently precise and certain for common inquirers to recognise in them a scientific character. The vulgar notion accordingly is, that all pretension to lay down general truths on politics and ,society is quackery; that no universality and no certainty are attainable in such matters. What partly excuses this common notion is, that it is really not without foundation in one particular sense. A large proportion of those who have laid claim to the character of philosophic politicians have attempted, not to ascertain universal sequences, but to frame universal precepts. They have imagined some one form of government, or system of laws, to fit all cases; a pretension well meriting the ridicule with which it is treated by practitioners, and wholly unsupported by the analogy of the art to which, from the nature of its subject, that of politics must be the most nearly allied. No one now supposes it possible that one remedy can cure all diseases, or even the same disease in all constitutions and habits of body.

It is not necessary even to the perfection of a science that the corresponding art should possess universal, or even general rules. The phenomena of society might not only be completely dependent on known causes, but the mode of action of all those causes might be reducible to laws of considerable simplicity, and yet no two cases might admit of being treated in precisely the same manner. So great might be the variety of circumstances on which the results in different cases depend, that the art might not have a single general precept to give, except that of watching the circumstances of the particular case, and adapting our measures to the effects which, according to the principles of the science, result from those circumstances. But although, in so complicated a class of subjects, it is impossible to lay down practical maxims of universal application, it does not follow that the phenomena do not conform to universal laws.

2. Of what nature the social science must be

All phenomena of society are phenomena of human nature, generated by the action of outward circumstances upon masses of human beings: and if, therefore, the phenomena of human thought, feeling, and action, are subject to fixed laws, the phenomena of society cannot but conform to fixed laws, the consequence of the preceding. There is, indeed, no hope that these laws, though our knowledge of them were as certain and as complete as it is in astronomy, would enable us to predict the history of society, like that of the celestial appearances, for thousands of years to come. But the difference of certainty is not in the laws themselves, it is in the data to which these laws are to be applied. In astronomy the causes influencing the result are few, and change little, and that little according to known laws; we can ascertain what they are now, and thence determine what they will be at any epoch of a distant future. The data, therefore, in astronomy, are as certain as the laws themselves. The circumstances, on the contrary, which influence the condition and progress of society, are innumerable, and perpetually changing; and though they all change in obedience to causes, and therefore to laws, the multitude of the causes is so great as to defy our limited powers of calculation. Not to say that the impossibility of applying precise numbers to facts of such a description, would set an impassable limit to the possibility of calculating them beforehand, even if the powers of the human intellect were otherwise adequate to the task.

But, as before remarked, an amount of knowledge quite insufficient for prediction may be most valuable for guidance. The science of society would have attained a very high point of perfection if it enabled us, in any given condition of social affairs, – in the condition, for instance, of Europe or any European country at the present time, – to understand by what causes it had, in any and every particular, been made what it was; whether it was tending to any, and to what, changes; what effects each feature of its existing state was likely to produce in the future; and by what means any of those effects might be prevented, modified, or accelerated, or a different class of effects superinduced. There is nothing chimerical in the hope that general laws, sufficient to enable us to answer these various questions for any country or time with the individual circumstances of which we are well acquainted, do really admit of being ascertained; and that the other branches of human knowledge, which this undertaking presupposes, are so far advanced that the time is ripe for its commencement. Such is the object of the Social Science.

That the nature of what I consider the true method of the science may be made more palpable, by first showing what that method is not, it will be expedient to characterise briefly two radical misconceptions of the proper mode of philosophising on society and government, one or other of which is, either explicitly or more often unconsciously, entertained by almost all who have meditated or argued respecting the logic of politics since the notion of treating it by strict rules, and on Baconian principles, has been current among the more advanced thinkers. These erroneous methods, if the word method can be applied to erroneous tendencies arising from the absence of any sufficiently distinct conception of method, may be termed the Experimental or Chemical mode of investigation, and the Abstract or Geometrical mode. We shall begin with the former.

CHAPTER SEVEN

Of the Chemical, or Experimental
Method in the Social Science

1. Characters of the mode of thinking which deduces political doctrines from
specific experience

The laws of the phenomena of society are, and can be, nothing but
the laws of the actions and passions of human beings united together
in the social state. Men, however, in a state of society, are still men;
their actions and passions are obedient to the laws of individual
human nature. Men are not, when brought together, converted into
another kind of substance, with different properties: as hydrogen
and oxygen are different from water, or as hydrogen, oxygen,
carbon, and azote are different from nerves, muscles, and tendons.
Human beings in society have no properties but those which are
derived from, and may be resolved into, the laws of the nature of
individual man. In social phenomena the Composition of Causes is
the universal law.

Now, the method of philosophising which may be termed
chemical overlooks this fact, and proceeds as if the nature of man as
an individual were not concerned at all, or were concerned in a very
inferior degree, in the operations of human beings in society. All
reasoning in political or social affairs, grounded on principles of
human nature, is objected to by reasoners of this sort, under such
names as 'abstract theory'. For the direction of their opinions and
conduct they profess to demand, in all cases without exception,
specific experience.

This mode of thinking is not only general with practitioners in
politics, and with that very numerous class who (on a subject which
no one, however ignorant, thinks himself incompetent to discuss)
profess to guide themselves by common sense rather than by science,

but is often countenanced by persons with great pretensions to instruction – persons who, having sufficient acquaintance with books and with the current ideas to have heard that Bacon taught mankind to follow experience, and to ground their conclusions on facts instead of metaphysical dogmas – think that, by treating political facts in as directly experimental a method as chemical facts, they are showing themselves true Baconians, and proving their adversaries to be mere syllogisers and schoolmen. As, however, the notion of the applicability of experimental methods to political philosophy cannot co-exist with any just conception of these methods themselves, the kind of arguments from experience which the chemical theory brings forth as its fruits (and which form the staple, in this country especially, of parliamentary and hustings oratory) are such as, at no time since Bacon, would have been admitted to be valid in chemistry itself, or in any other branch of experimental science. They are such as these: that the prohibition of foreign commodities must conduce to national wealth, because England has flourished under it, or because countries in general which have adopted it have flourished; that our laws, or our internal administration, or our constitution, are excellent for a similar reason; and the eternal arguments from historical examples, from Athens or Rome, from the fires in Smithfield or the French Revolution.

I will not waste time in contending against modes of argumentation which no person, with the smallest practice in estimating evidence, could possibly be betrayed into; which draw conclusions of general application from a single unanalysed instance, or arbitrarily refer an effect to some one among its antecedents, without any process of elimination or comparison of instances. It is a rule both of justice and of good sense to grapple not with the absurdest, but with the most reasonable form of a wrong opinion. We shall suppose our inquirer acquainted with the true conditions of experimental investigation, and competent in point of acquirements for realising them, so far as they can be realised. He shall know as much of the facts of history as mere erudition can teach – as much as can be proved by testimony without the assistance of any theory; and if those mere facts, properly collated, can fulfil the conditions of a real induction, he shall be qualified for the task.

But that no such attempt can have the smallest chance of success, has been abundantly shown in the tenth chapter of the Third Book.

We there examined whether effects which depend on a complication of causes can be made the subject of a true induction by observation and experiment; and concluded, on the most convincing grounds, that they cannot. Since, of all effects, none depend on so great a complication of causes as social phenomena, we might leave our case to rest in safety on that previous showing. But a logical principle as yet so little familiar to the ordinary run of thinkers requires to be insisted on more than once in order to make the due impression; and the present being the case which of all others exemplifies it the most strongly, there will be advantage in re-stating the grounds of the general maxim, as applied to the specialities of the class of inquiries now under consideration.

2. In the social science experiments are impossible

The first difficulty which meets us in the attempt to apply experimental methods for ascertaining the laws of social phenomena, is that we are without the means of making artificial experiments. Even if we could contrive experiments at leisure, and try them without limit, we should do so under immense disadvantage; both from the impossibility of ascertaining and taking note of all the facts of each case, and because (those facts being in a perpetual state of change) before sufficient time had elapsed to ascertain the result of the experiment, some material circumstances would always have ceased to be the same. But it is unnecessary to consider the logical objections which would exist to the conclusiveness of our experiments, since we palpably never have the power of trying any. We can only watch those which nature produces, or which are produced for other reasons. We cannot adapt our logical means to our wants by varying the circumstances as the exigencies of elimination may require. If the spontaneous instances formed by contemporary events and by the successions of phenomena recorded in history afford a sufficient variation of circumstances, an induction from specific experience is attainable; otherwise not. The question to be resolved is, therefore, whether the requisites for induction respecting the causes of political effects or the properties of political agents are to be met with in history? including under the term contemporary history. And in order to give fixity to our conceptions, it will be advisable to suppose this question asked in reference to some special subject of political inquiry or controversy; such as that frequent topic of debate in the present century, the operation of restrictive and prohibitory commercial legislation upon national wealth. Let this, then, be the scientific question to be investigated by specific experience.

3. The method of difference is inexplicable

In order to apply to the case the most perfect of the methods of experimental inquiry, the Method of Difference, we require to find two instances which tally in every particular except the one which is the subject of inquiry. If two nations can be found which are alike in all natural advantages and disadvantages; whose people resemble each other in every quality, physical and moral, spontaneous and acquired; whose habits, usages, opinions, laws and institutions are the same in all respects, except that one of them has a more protective tariff, or in other respects interferes more with the freedom of industry; if one of these nations is found to be rich and the other poor, or one richer than the other, this will be an *experimentum crucis* – a real proof by experience which of the two systems is most favourable to national riches. But the supposition that two such instances can be met with is manifestly absurd. Nor is such a concurrence even abstractedly possible. Two nations which agreed in everything except their commercial policy would agree also in that. Differences of legislation are not inherent and ultimate diversities – are not properties of Kinds. They are effects of pre-existing causes. If the two nations differ in this portion of their institutions, it is from some difference in their position, and thence in their apparent interests, or in some portion or other of their opinions, habits and tendencies; which opens a view of further differences without any assignable limit, capable of operating on their industrial prosperity, as well as on every other feature of their condition, in more ways than can be enumerated or imagined. There is thus a demonstrated impossibility of obtaining, in the investigations of the social science, the conditions required for the most conclusive form of inquiry by specific experience.

In the absence of the direct, we may next try, as in other cases, the supplementary resource, called in a former place the Indirect Method of Difference, which, instead of two instances differing in nothing but the presence or absence of a given circumstance, compares two *classes* of instances respectively agreeing in nothing but the presence of a circumstance on the one side and its absence on the other. To choose the most advantageous case conceivable, (a case far too advantageous to be ever obtained,) suppose that we compare one nation which has a restrictive policy, with two or more nations agreeing in nothing but in permitting free trade. We need not now suppose that either of these nations agrees with the first in all its circumstances; one may agree with it in some of its circumstances, and another in the remainder. And it may be argued, that if these nations remain poorer than the restrictive nation, it cannot be for want either of the first or of the second set of circumstances, but it must be for want of the protective system. If (we might say) the restrictive nation had prospered from the one set of causes, the first of the free-trade nations would have prospered equally: if, by reason of the other, the second would: but neither has: therefore the prosperity was owing to the restrictions. This will be allowed to be a very favourable specimen of an argument from specific experience in politics, and if this be inconclusive, it would not be easy to find another preferable to it.

Yet that it is inconclusive scarcely requires to be pointed out. Why must the prosperous nation have prospered from one cause exclusively? National prosperity is always the collective result of a multitude of favourable circumstances; and of these, the restrictive nation may unite a greater number than either of the others, though it may have all of those circumstances in common with either one or the other of them. Its prosperity may be partly owing to circumstances common to it with one of those nations, and partly with the other, while they, having each of them only half the number of favourable circumstances, have remained inferior. So that the closest imitation which can be made in the social science of a legitimate induction from direct experience gives but a specious semblance of conclusiveness, without any real value.

4. The methods of agreement and of concomitant variations are inconclusive

The Method of Difference in either of its forms being thus completely out of the question, there remains the Method of Agreement. But we are already aware of how little value this method is in cases admitting Plurality of Causes; and social phenomena are those in which the plurality prevails in the utmost possible extent.

Suppose that the observer makes the luckiest hit which could be given by any conceivable combination of chances: that he finds two nations which agree in no circumstance whatever, except in having a restrictive system and in being prosperous; or a number of nations, all prosperous, which have no antecedent circumstances common to them all but that of having a restrictive policy. It is unnecessary to go into the consideration of the impossibility of ascertaining from history, or even from contemporary observation, that such is really the fact: that the nations agree in no other circumstance capable of influencing the case. Let us suppose this impossibility vanquished, and the fact ascertained that they agree only in a restrictive system as an antecedent, and industrial prosperity as a consequent. What degree of presumption does this raise, that the restrictive system caused the prosperity? One so trifling as to be equivalent to none at all. That some one antecedent is the cause of a given effect, because all other antecedents have been found capable of being eliminated, is a just inference only if the effect can have but one cause. If it admits of several, nothing is more natural than that each of these should separately admit of being eliminated. Now, in the case of political phenomena, the supposition of unity of cause is not only wide of the truth, but at an immeasurable distance from it. The causes of every social phenomenon which we are particularly interested about, security, wealth, freedom, good government, public virtue, general intelligence, or their opposites, are infinitely numerous, especially the external or remote causes, which alone are, for the most part, accessible to direct observation. No one cause suffices of itself to produce any of these phenomena; while there are countless causes which have some influence over them, and may co-operate either in their production or in their prevention. From the mere fact, therefore, of our having been able to eliminate some circumstance, we can by no means infer that this circumstance was not instrumental to the effect in some of the very instances from which we have eliminated it. We can conclude that the effect is sometimes produced without it, but not that, when present, it does not contribute its share.

Similar objections will be found to apply to the Method of Concomitant Variations. If the causes which act upon the state of any society produced effects differing from one another in kind; if wealth depended on one cause, peace on another, a third made people virtuous, a fourth intelligent, we might, though unable to sever the causes from one another, refer to each of them that property of the effect which waxed as it waxed, and which waned as it waned. But every attribute of the social body is influenced by innumerable causes; and such is the mutual action of the co-existing elements of society, that whatever affects any one of the more important of them, will by that alone, if it does not affect the others directly, affect them indirectly. The effects, therefore, of different agents not being different in quality, while the quantity of each is the mixed result of all the agents, the variations of the aggregate cannot bear an uniform proportion to those of any one of its component parts.

5. *The method of residues is also inconclusive and presupposes deduction*

There remains the Method of Residues, which appears, on the first view, less foreign to this kind of inquiry than the three other methods, because it only requires that we should accurately note the circumstances of some one country, or state of society. Making allowance, thereupon, for the effect of all causes whose tendencies are known, the residue which those causes are inadequate to explain may plausibly be imputed to the remainder of the circumstances which are known to have existed in the case. Something similar to this is the method which Coleridge* describes himself as having followed in his political Essays in the *Morning Post*:

> On every great occurrence I endeavoured to discover in past history the event that most nearly resembled it. I procured, whenever it was possible, the contemporary historians, memorialists, and pamphleteers. Then fairly subtracting the points of difference from those of likeness, as the balance favoured the former or the latter, I conjectured that the result would be the same or different. As, for instance, in the series of essays entitled 'A Comparison of France under Napoleon with Rome under the first Caesars', and in those which followed, 'on the probable final restoration of the Bourbons'. The same plan I pursued at the commencement of the Spanish Revolution, and with the same success, taking the war of the United Provinces with Philip II. as the groundwork of the comparison.

In this inquiry he no doubt employed the Method of Residues, for, in

* *Biographia Literaria* i. 214.

'subtracting the points of difference from those of likeness', he doubtless weighed, and did not content himself with numbering, them: he doubtless took those points of agreement only which he presumed from their own nature to be capable of influencing the effect, and, allowing for that influence, concluded that the remainder of the result would be referable to the points of difference.

Whatever may be the efficacy of this method, it is, as we long ago remarked, not a method of pure observation and experiment; it concludes, not from a comparison of instances, but from the comparison of an instance with the result of a previous deduction. Applied to social phenomena, it presupposes that the causes from which part of the effect proceeded are already known; and as we have shown that these cannot have been known by specific experience, they must have been learnt by deduction from principles of human nature, experience being called in only as a supplementary resource, to determine the causes which produced an unexplained residue. But if the principles of human nature may be had recourse to for the establishment of some political truths, they may for all. If it be admissible to say, England must have prospered by reason of the prohibitory system, because after allowing for all the other tendencies which have been operating, there is a portion of prosperity still to be accounted for; it must be admissible to go to the same source for the effect of the prohibitory system, and examine what account the laws of human motives and actions will enable us to give of *its* tendencies. Nor, in fact, will the experimental argument amount to anything, except in verification of a conclusion drawn from those general laws. For we may subtract the effect of one, two, three, or four causes, but we shall never succeed in subtracting the effect of all causes except one; while it would be a curious instance of the dangers of too much caution, if, to avoid depending on *à priori* reasoning concerning the effect of a single cause, we should oblige ourselves to depend on as many separate *à priori* reasonings as there are causes operating concurrently with that particular cause in some given instance.

We have now sufficiently characterised the gross misconception of the mode of investigation proper to political phenomena, which I have termed the Chemical Method. So lengthened a discussion would not have been necessary if the claim to decide authoritatively on political doctrines were confined to persons who had competently studied any one of the higher departments of physical science. But since the generality of those who reason on political subjects, satisfactorily to themselves and to a more or less numerous body of admirers, know nothing whatever of the methods of physical investigation beyond a few precepts which they continue to parrot after Bacon, being entirely unaware that Bacon's conception of scientific inquiry has done its work, and that science has now advanced into a higher stage, there are probably many to whom such remarks as the foregoing may still be useful. In an age in which chemistry itself, when attempting to deal with the more complex chemical sequences, those of the animal, or even the vegetable organism, has found it necessary to become, and has succeeded in becoming, a Deductive Science, it is not to be apprehended that any person of scientific habits, who has kept pace with the general progress of the knowledge of nature, can be in danger of applying the methods of elementary chemistry to explore the sequences of the most complex order of phenomena in existence.

CHAPTER EIGHT

Of the Geometrical, or Abstract Method

1. *Characters of this mode of thinking*

The misconception discussed in the preceding chapter is, as we said, chiefly committed by persons not much accustomed to scientific investigation: practitioners in politics, who rather employ the commonplaces of philosophy to justify their practice, than seek to guide their practice by philosophic principles: or imperfectly educated persons, who, in ignorance of the careful selection and elaborate comparison of instances required for the formation of a sound theory, attempt to found one upon a few coincidences which they have casually noticed.

The erroneous method of which we are now to treat, is, on the contrary, peculiar to thinking and studious minds. It never could have suggested itself but to persons of some familiarity with the nature of scientific research; who, – being aware of the impossibility of establishing, by casual observation or direct experimentation, a true theory of sequences so complex as are those of the social phenomena, – have recourse to the simpler laws which are immediately operative in those phenomena, and which are no other than the laws of the nature of the human beings therein concerned. These thinkers perceive (what the partisans of the chemical or experimental theory do not) that the science of society must necessarily be deductive. But, from an insufficient consideration of the specific nature of the subject-matter, – and often because (their own scientific education having stopped short in too early a stage) geometry stands in their minds as the type of all deductive science, – it is to geometry, rather than to astronomy and natural philosophy, that they unconsciously assimilate the deductive science of society.

Among the differences between geometry (a science of co-existent facts, altogether independent of the laws of the succession of phenomena) and those physical Sciences of Causation which have been rendered deductive, the following is one of the most conspicuous: That geometry affords no room for what so constantly occurs in mechanics and its applications, the case of conflicting forces; of causes which counteract or modify one another. In mechanics we continually find two or more moving forces producing, not motion, but rest; or motion in a different direction from that which would have been produced by either of the generating forces. It is true that the effect of the joint forces is the same when they act simultaneously, as if they had acted one after another, or by turns; and it is in this that the difference between mechanical and chemical law consists. But still the effects, whether produced by successive or by simultaneous action, do, wholly or in part, cancel one another: what the one force does the other, partly or altogether, undoes. There is no similar state of things in geometry. The result which follows from one geometrical principle has nothing that conflicts with the result which follows from another. What is proved true from one geometrical theorem, what would be true if no other geometrical principles existed, cannot be altered and made no longer true by reason of some other geometrical principle. What is once proved true is true in all cases, whatever supposition may be made in regard to any other matter.

Now a conception, similar to this last, would appear to have been formed of the social science, in the minds of the earlier of those who have attempted to cultivate it by a deductive method. Mechanics would be a science very similar to geometry if every motion resulted from one force alone, and not from a conflict of forces. In the geometrical theory of society, it seems to be supposed that this is really the case with the social phenomena; that each of them results always from only one force, one single property of human nature.

At the point which we have now reached, it cannot be necessary to say anything either in proof or in illustration of the assertion that such is not the true character of the social phenomena. There is not, among these most complex and (for that reason) most modifiable of all phenomena, any one over which innumerable forces do not exercise influence; which does not depend on a conjunction of very many causes. We have not, therefore, to prove the notion in question to be an error, but to prove that the error has been committed; that so mistaken a conception of the mode in which the phenomena of society are produced has actually been ascertained.

2. *Examples of the geometrical method*

One numerous division of the reasoners who have treated social facts according to geometrical methods, not admitting any modification of one law by another, must for the present be left out of consideration; because in them this error is complicated with and is the effect of another fundamental misconception, of which we have already taken some notice, and which will be further treated of before we conclude. I speak of those who deduce political conclusions not from laws of nature, not from sequences of phenomena, real or imaginary, but from unbending practical maxims. Such, for example, are all who found their theory of politics on what is called abstract right, that is to say, on universal precepts; a pretension of which we have already noticed the chimerical nature. Such, in like manner, are those who make the assumption of a social contract, or any other kind of original obligation, and apply it to particular cases by mere interpretation. But in this the fundamental error is the attempt to treat an art like a science, and to have a deductive art; the irrationality of which will be shown in a future chapter. It will be proper to take our exemplification of the geometrical theory from those thinkers who have avoided this additional error, and who entertain, so far, a juster idea of the nature of political inquiry.

We may cite, in the first instance, those who assume as the principle of their political philosophy that government is founded on fear; that the dread of each other is the one motive by which human beings were originally brought into a state of society, and are still held in it. Some of the earlier scientific inquirers into politics, in particular Hobbes, assumed this proposition, not by implication, but avowedly, as the foundation of their doctrine, and attempted to build a complete philosophy of politics thereupon. It is true that Hobbes did not find this one maxim sufficient to carry him through the whole of his subject, but was obliged to eke it out by the double sophism of an original contract. I call this a double sophism; first, as passing off a fiction for a fact, and, secondly, assuming a practical principle or precept as the basis of a theory; which is a *petitio principii*, since (as we noticed in treating of that Fallacy) every rule of conduct, even though it be so binding a one as the observance of a promise, must rest its own foundations on the theory of the subject, and the theory, therefore, cannot rest upon it.

3. *The interest-philosophy of the Bentham School*

Passing over less important instances, I shall come at once to the most remarkable example afforded by our own times of the geometrical method in politics; emanating from persons who are well aware of the distinction between science and art; who know that rules of conduct must follow, not precede, the ascertainment of laws of nature, and that the latter, not the former, is the legitimate field for the application of the deductive method. I allude to the interest-philosophy of the Bentham School.

The profound and original thinkers who are commonly known under this description, founded their general theory of government on one comprehensive premise, namely, that men's actions are always determined by their interests. There is an ambiguity in this last expression; for, as the same philosophers, especially Bentham, gave the name of an interest to anything which a person likes, the proposition may be understood to mean only this, that men's actions are always determined by their wishes. In this sense, however, it would not bear out any of the consequences which these writers drew from it; and the word, therefore, in their political reasonings, must be understood to mean (which is also the explanation they themselves, on such occasions, gave of it) what is commonly termed private or worldly interest.

Taking the doctrine, then, in this sense, an objection presents itself *in limine* which might be deemed a fatal one, namely, that so sweeping a proposition is far from being universally true. Human beings are not governed in all their actions by their worldly interests. This, however, is by no means so conclusive an objection as it at first appears; because in politics we are for the most part concerned with the conduct, not of individual persons, but either of a series of persons (as a succession of kings), or a body or mass of persons, as a nation, an aristocracy, or a representative assembly. And whatever is true of a large majority of mankind, may without much error be taken for true of any succession of persons, considered as a whole, or of any collection of persons in which the act of the majority becomes the act of the whole body. Although, therefore, the maxim is sometimes expressed in a manner unnecessarily paradoxical, the consequences drawn from it will hold equally good if the assertion be limited as follows: Any succession of persons, or the majority of any body of persons, will be governed in the bulk of their conduct by their personal interests. We are bound to allow to this school of thinkers the benefit of this more rational statement of their fundamental maxim, which is also in strict conformity to the explanations which, when considered to be called for, have been given by themselves.

The theory goes on to infer, quite correctly, that if the actions of mankind are determined in the main by their selfish interests, the only rulers who will govern according to the interest of the governed are those whose selfish interests are in accordance with it. And to this is added a third proposition, namely, that no rulers have their selfish interest identical with that of the governed, unless it be rendered so by accountability, that is, by dependence on the will of the governed. In other words (and as the result of the whole), that the desire of retaining or the fear of losing their power, and whatever is thereon consequent, is the sole motive which can be relied on for producing on the part of rulers a course of conduct in accordance with the general interest.

We have thus a fundamental theorem of political science, consisting of three syllogisms, and depending chiefly on two general premises, in each of which a certain effect is considered as determined only by the one cause, not by a concurrence of causes. In the one, it is assumed that the actions of average rulers are determined solely by self-interest; in the other, that the sense of identity of interest with the governed, is produced and producible by no other cause than responsibility.

Neither of these propositions is by any means true; the last is extremely wide of the truth.

It is not true that the actions even of average rulers are wholly, or anything approaching to wholly, determined by their personal interest, or even by their own opinion of their personal interest. I do not speak of the influence of a sense of duty, or feelings of philanthropy, motives never to be mainly relied on, though (except in countries or during periods of great moral debasement) they influence almost all rulers in some degree, and some rulers in a very great degree. But I insist only on what is true of all rulers, viz. that the character and course of their actions is largely influenced (independently of personal calculation) by the habitual sentiments and feelings, the general modes of thinking and acting, which prevail throughout the community of which they are members, as well as by the feelings, habits and modes of thought which characterise the particular class in that community to which they themselves belong. And no one will understand or be able to decipher their system of conduct who does not take all these things into account. They are also much influenced by the maxims and traditions which have descended to them from other rulers, their predecessors; which maxims and traditions have been known to retain an ascendancy during long periods, even in opposition to the private interests of the rulers for the time being. I put aside the influence of other less general causes. Although, therefore, the private interests of the rulers or of the ruling class is a very powerful force, constantly in action, and exercising the most important influence upon their conduct, there is also in what they do a large portion which that private interest by no means affords a sufficient explanation of; and even the particulars which constitute the goodness or badness of their government are in some, and no small degree, influenced by those among the circumstances acting upon them, which cannot, with any propriety, be included in the term self-interest.

Turning now to the other proposition, that responsibility to the governed is the only cause capable of producing in the rulers a sense of identity of interest with community; this is still less admissible as an universal truth, than even the former. I am not speaking of perfect identity of interest, which is an impracticable chimera, which, most assuredly, responsibility to the people does not give. I speak of identity in essentials; and the essentials are different at different places and times. There are a large number of cases in which those things which it is most for the general interest that the rulers should do, are also those which they are prompted to do by their strongest personal interest, the consolidation of their power. The suppression, for instance, of anarchy and resistance to law, – the complete establishment of the authority of the central government, in a state of society like that of Europe in the middle ages, – is one of the strongest interests of the people, and also of the rulers simply because they are the rulers: and responsibility on their part could not strengthen, though in many conceivable ways it might weaken, the motives prompting them to pursue this object. During the greater part of the reign of Queen Elizabeth, and of many other monarchs who might be named, the sense of identity of interest between the sovereign and the majority of the people was probably stronger than it usually is in responsible governments: everything that the people had most at heart, the monarch had at heart too. Had Peter the Great, or the rugged savages whom he began to civilise, the truest inclination towards the things which were for the real interest of those savages?

I am not here attempting to establish a theory of government, and am not called upon to determine the proportional weight which ought to be given to the circumstances which this school of geometrical politicians left out of their system, and those which they took into it. I am only concerned to show that their method was unscientific; not to measure the amount of error which may have affected their practical conclusions.

It is but justice to them, however, to remark that their mistake was not so much one of substance as of form; and consisted in presenting in a systematic shape, and as the scientific treatment of a great philosophical question, what should have passed for that which it really was, the mere polemics of the day. Although the actions of rulers are by no means wholly determined by their selfish interests, it is chiefly as a security against those selfish interests that constitutional checks are required; and for that purpose such checks, in England, and the other nations of modern Europe, can in no manner be dispensed with. It is likewise true, that in these same nations, and in the present age, responsibility to the governed is the only means practically available to create a feeling of identity of interest, in the cases, and on the points, where that feeling does not sufficiently exist. To all this, and to the arguments which may be founded on it in favour of measures for the correction of our representative system, I have nothing to object; but I confess my regret, that the small though highly important portion of the philosophy of government, which was wanted for the immediate purpose of serving the cause of parliamentary reform, should have been held forth by thinkers of such eminence as a complete theory.

It is not to be imagined possible, nor is it true in point of fact, that these philosophers regarded the few premises of their theory as including all that is required for explaining social phenomena, or for determining the choice of forms of government and measures of legislation and administration. They were too highly instructed, of too comprehensive intellect, and some of them of too sober and practical a character, for such an error. They would have applied, and did apply, their principles with innumerable allowances. But it is not allowances that are wanted. There is little chance of making due amends in the superstructure of a theory for the want of sufficient breadth in its foundations. It is unphilosophical to construct a science out of a few of the agencies by which the phenomena are determined, and leave the rest to the routine of practice or the sagacity of conjecture. We either ought not to pretend to scientific forms, or we ought to study all the determining agencies equally, and endeavour, so far as it can be done, to include all of them within the pale of the science; else we shall infallibly bestow a disproportionate attention upon those which our theory takes into account, while we misestimate the rest, and probably underrate their importance. That the deductions should be from the whole and not from a part only of the laws of nature that are concerned, would be desirable even if those omitted were so insignificant in comparison with the others, that they might, for most purposes and on most occasions, be left out of the account. But this is far indeed from being true in the social science. The phenomena of society do not depend, in essentials, on some one agency or law of human nature, with only inconsiderable modifications from others. The whole of the qualities of human nature influence those phenomena, and there is not one which influences them in a small degree. There is not one, the removal or any great alteration of which would not materially affect the whole aspect of society, and change more or less the sequences of social phenomena generally.

The theory which has been the subject of these remarks is, in this country at least, the principal contemporary example of what I have styled the geometrical method of philosophising in the social science; and our examination of it has, for this reason, been more detailed than would otherwise have been suitable to a work like the present. Having now sufficiently illustrated the two erroneous methods, we shall pass without further preliminary to the true method; that which proceeds (conformably to the practice of the more complex physical sciences) deductively indeed, but by deduction from many, not from one or a very few, original premises; considering each effect as (what it really is) an aggregate result of many causes, operating sometimes through the same, sometimes through different mental agencies, or laws of human nature.

CHAPTER NINE

Of the Physical, or
Concrete Deductive Method

1. The direct and inverse deductive methods

After what has been said to illustrate the nature of the inquiry into social phenomena, the general character of the method proper to that inquiry is sufficiently evident, and needs only to be recapitulated, not proved. However complex the phenomena, all their sequences and co-existences result from the laws of the separate elements. The effect produced, in social phenomena, by any complex set of circumstances, amounts precisely to the sum of the effects of the circumstances taken singly; and the complexity does not arise from the number of the laws themselves, which is not remarkably great, but from the extraordinary number and variety of the data or elements – of the agents which, in obedience to that small number of laws, co-operate towards the effect. The Social Science, therefore, (which, by a convenient barbarism, has been termed Sociology) is a deductive science; not, indeed, after the model of geometry, but after that of the more complex physical sciences. It infers the law of each effect from the laws of causation on which that effect depends; not, however, from the law merely of one cause, as in the geometrical method; but by considering all the causes which conjunctly influence the effect, and compounding their laws with one another. Its method, in short, is the Concrete Deductive Method; that of which astronomy furnishes the most perfect, natural philosophy a somewhat less perfect example, and the employment of which, with the adaptations and precautions required by the subject, is beginning to regenerate physiology.

Nor does it admit of doubt that similar adaptations and precautions are indispensable in sociology. In applying to that most complex of all studies what is demonstrably the sole method capable of throwing the light of science even upon phenomena of a far inferior degree of complication, we ought to be aware that the same superior complexity which renders the instrument of deduction more necessary, renders it also more precarious; and we must be prepared to meet, by appropriate contrivances, this increase of difficulty.

The actions and feelings of human beings in the social state are, no doubt, entirely governed by psychological and ethological laws; whatever influence any cause exercises upon the social phenomena, it exercises through those laws. Supposing, therefore, the laws of human actions and feelings to be sufficiently known, there is no extraordinary difficulty in determining from those laws the nature of the social effects which any given cause tends to produce. But when the question is that of compounding several tendencies together, and computing the aggregate result of many co-existent causes; and especially when, by attempting to predict what will actually occur in a given case, we incur the obligation of estimating and compounding the influences of all the causes which happen to exist in that case; we attempt a task to proceed far in which surpasses the compass of the human faculties.

If all the resources of science are not sufficient to enable us to calculate *à priori*, with complete precision, the mutual action of three bodies gravitating towards one another; it may be judged with what prospect of success we should endeavour to calculate the result of the conflicting tendencies which are acting in a thousand different directions and promoting a thousand different changes at a given instant in a given society: although we might and ought to be able, from the laws of human nature, to distinguish correctly enough the tendencies themselves, so far as they depend on causes accessible to our observation; and determine the direction which each of them, if acting alone, would impress upon society, as well as, in a general way at least, to pronounce that some of these tendencies are more powerful than others.

But, without dissembling the necessary imperfections of the *à priori* method when applied to such a subject, neither ought we, on the other hand, to exaggerate them. The same objections which apply to the Method of Deduction in this its most difficult employment, apply to it, as we formerly showed, * in its easiest; and would even there have been insuperable, if there had not existed, as was then fully explained, an appropriate remedy. This remedy consists in the process which, under the name of Verification, we have characterised as the third essential constituent part of the Deductive Method; that of collating the conclusion of the ratiocination either with the concrete phenomena themselves, or, when such are obtainable, with their empirical laws. The ground of confidence in any concrete deductive science is not the *à priori* reasoning itself, but the accordance between its results and those of observation *à posteriori*. Either of these processes, apart from the other, diminishes in value as the subject increases in complication, and this in so rapid a ratio as soon to become entirely worthless; but the reliance to be placed in the concurrence of the two sorts of evidence not only does not diminish in anything like the same proportion, but is not necessarily much diminished at all. Nothing more results than a disturbance in the order of precedency of the two processes, sometimes amounting to its actual inversion: insomuch that, instead of deducing our conclusions by reasoning, and verifying them by observation, we in some cases begin by obtaining them provisionally from specific experience, and afterwards connect them with the principles of human nature by *à priori* reasonings, which reasonings are thus a real Verification.

The only thinker who, with a competent knowledge of scientific methods in general, has attempted to characterise the Method of Sociology, M. Comte, considers this inverse order as inseparably inherent in the nature of sociological speculation. He looks upon the social science as essentially consisting of generalisations from history, verified, not originally suggested, by deduction from the laws of human nature. Though there is a truth contained in this opinion, of which I shall presently endeavour to show the importance, I cannot but think that this truth is enunciated in too unlimited a manner, and that there is considerable scope in sociological inquiry for the direct, as well as for the inverse, Deductive Method.

It will, in fact, be shown in the next chapter, that there is a kind of sociological inquiries to which, from their prodigious complication, the method of direct deduction is altogether inapplicable, while by a happy compensation it is precisely in these cases that we are able to obtain the best empirical laws: to these inquiries, therefore, the

---

* Book III, Chap. x, §7.

Inverse Method is exclusively adapted. But there are also, as will presently appear, other cases in which it is impossible to obtain from direct observation anything worthy the name of an empirical law; and it fortunately happens that these are the very cases in which the Direct Method is least affected by the objection, which undoubtedly must always affect it in a certain degree.

We shall begin, then, by looking at the Social Science as a science of direct Deduction, and considering what can be accomplished in it, and under what limitations, by that mode of investigation. We shall, then, in a separate chapter, examine and endeavour to characterise the inverse process.

2. *Difficulties of the direct deductive method in the social science*

It is evident, in the first place, that Sociology, considered as a system of deductions *à priori*, cannot be a science of positive predictions, but only of tendencies. We may be able to conclude, from the laws of human nature applied to the circumstances of a given state of society, that a particular cause will operate in a certain manner unless counteracted; but we can never be assured to what extent or amount it will so operate, or affirm with certainty that it will not be counteracted; because we can seldom know, even approximately, all the agencies which may co-exist with it, and still less calculate the collective result of so many combined elements. The remark, however, must here be once more repeated, that knowledge insufficient for prediction may be most valuable for guidance. It is not necessary for the wise conduct of the affairs of society, no more than of any one's private concerns, that we should be able to foresee infallibly the results of what we do. We must seek our objects by means which may perhaps be defeated, and take precautions against dangers which possibly may never be realised. The aim of practical politics is to surround any given society with the greatest possible number of circumstances of which the tendencies are beneficial, and to remove or counteract, as far as practicable, those of which the tendencies are injurious. A knowledge of the tendencies only, though without the power of accurately predicting their conjunct result, gives us to a considerable extent this power.

It would, however, be an error to suppose that, even with respect to tendencies, we could arrive in this manner at any great number of propositions which will be true in all societies without exception. Such a supposition would be inconsistent with the eminently modifiable nature of the social phenomena, and the multitude and variety of the circumstances by which they are modified; circumstances are never the same, or even nearly the same, in two different societies, or in two different periods of the same society. This would not be so serious an obstacle if, though the causes acting upon society in general are numerous, those which influence any one feature of society were limited in number; for we might then insulate any particular social phenomenon, and investigate its laws without disturbance from the rest. But the truth is the very opposite of this. Whatever affects, in an appreciable degree, any one element of the social state, affects through it all the other elements. The mode of production of all social phenomena is one great case of Intermixture of Laws. We can never either understand in theory or command in practice the condition of a society in any one respect, without taking into consideration its condition in all other respects. There is no social phenomenon which is not more or less influenced by every other part of the condition of the same society, and therefore by every cause which is influencing any other of the contemporaneous social phenomena. There is, in short, what physiologists term a *consensus*, similar to that existing among the various organs and functions of the physical frame of man and the more perfect animals, and constituting one of the many analogies which have rendered universal such expressions as the 'body politic' and 'body natural'. It follows from this *consensus*, that unless two societies could be alike in all the circumstances which surround and influence them, (which would imply their being alike in their previous history,) no portion whatever of the phenomena will, unless by accident, precisely correspond; no one cause will produce exactly the same effects in both. Every cause, as its effect spreads through society, comes somewhere in contact with different sets of agencies, and thus has its effects on some of the social phenomena differently modified; and these differences, by their reaction, produce a difference even in those of the effects which would otherwise have been the same. We can never, therefore, affirm with certainty that a cause which has a particular tendency in one people or in one age will have exactly the same tendency in another, without referring back to our premises, and performing over again for the second age or nation that analysis of the whole of its influencing circumstances which we had already performed for the first. The deductive science of society will not lay down a theorem, asserting in an universal manner the effect of any cause; but will rather teach us how to frame the proper theorem for the circumstances of any given case. It will not give the laws of society in general, but the means of determining the phenomena of any given society from the particular elements or data of that society.

All the general propositions which can be framed by the deductive science are, therefore, in the strictest sense of the word, hypothetical. They are grounded on some suppositious set of circumstances, and declare how some given cause would operate in those circumstances, supposing that no others were combined with them. If the set of circumstances supposed have been copied from those of any existing society, the conclusions will be true of that society, provided, and in as far as, the effect of those circumstances shall not be modified by others which have not been taken into the account. If we desire a nearer approach to concrete truth, we can only aim at it by taking, or endeavouring to take, a greater number of individualising circumstances into the computation.

Considering, however, in how accelerating a ratio the uncertainty of our conclusions increase as we attempt to take the effect of a greater number of concurrent causes into our calculations, the hypothetical combinations of circumstances on which we construct the general theorem of the science cannot be made very complex without so rapidly accumulating a liability to error as must soon deprive our conclusions of all value. This mode of inquiry, considered as a means of obtaining general propositions, must therefore, on pain of frivolity, be limited to those classes of social facts which, though influenced like the rest by all sociological agents, are under the *immediate* influence, principally at least, of a few only.

3. To what extent the different branches of sociological speculation can be studied apart. Political economy characterised

Notwithstanding the universal *consensus* of the social phenomena, whereby nothing which takes place in any part of the operations of society is without its share of influence on every other part; and notwithstanding the paramount ascendancy which the general start of civilisation and social progress in any given society must hence exercise over all the partial and subordinate phenomena; it is not the less true that different species of social facts are in the main dependent, immediately and in the first resort, on different kinds of causes; and therefore not only may with advantage, but must, be studied apart: just as in the natural body we study separately the physiology and pathology of each of the principal organs and tissues, though every one is acted upon by the state of all the others; and though the peculiar constitution and general state of health of the organism co-operates with, and often preponderates over, the local causes, in determining the state of any particular organ.

On these considerations is grounded the existence of distinct and separate, though not independent, branches or departments of sociological speculation.

There is, for example, one large class of social phenomena in which the immediately determining causes are principally those which act through the desire of wealth, and in which the psychological law mainly concerned is the familiar one that a greater gain is preferred to a smaller. I mean, of course, that portion of the phenomena of society which emanates from the industrial or productive operations of mankind, and from those of their acts through which the distribution of the products of those industrial operations take place, in so far as not effected by force or modified by voluntary gift. By reasoning from that one law of human nature, and from the principal outward circumstances (whether universal or confined to particular states of society) which operate upon the human mind through that law, we may be enabled to explain and predict this portion of the phenomena of society, so far as they depend on that class of circumstances only, overlooking the influence of any other of the circumstances of society, and therefore neither tracing back the circumstances which we do take into account to their possible origin in some other facts in the social state, nor making allowance for the manner in which any of those other circumstances may interfere with and counteract or modify the effect of the former. A department of science may thus be constructed, which has received the name of Political Economy.

The motive which suggests the separation of this portion of the social phenomena from the rest, and the creation of a distinct branch of science relating to them, is, that they do *mainly* depend, at least in the first resort, on one class of circumstances only; and that even when other circumstances interfere, the ascertainment of the effect due to the one class of circumstances alone is a sufficiently intricate and difficult business to make it expedient to perform it once for all, and then allow for the effect of the modifying circumstances; especially as certain fixed combinations of the former are apt to recur often, in conjunction with ever-varying circumstances of the latter class.

Political Economy, as I have said on another occasion, concerns itself only with

such of the phenomena of the social state as take place in consequence of the pursuit of wealth. It makes entire abstraction of every other human passion or motive, except those which may be regarded as perpetually antagonising principles to the desire of wealth, namely, aversion to labour, and desire of the present enjoyment of costly indulgences. These it takes, to a certain extent, into its calculations, because these do not merely, like our other desires, occasionally conflict with the pursuit of wealth, but accompany it always as a drag or impediment, and are therefore inseparably mixed up in the consideration of it. Political Economy considers mankind as occupied solely in acquiring and consuming wealth, and aims at showing what is the course of action into which mankind, living in a state of society, would be impelled if that motive, except in the degree in which it is checked by the two perpetual counter-motives above adverted to, were absolute ruler of all their actions. Under the influence of this desire, it shows mankind accumulating wealth, and employing that wealth in the production of other wealth; sanctioning by mutual agreement the institution of property; establishing laws to prevent individuals from encroaching upon the property of others by force or fraud; adopting various contrivances for increasing the productiveness of their labour; settling the division of the produce by agreement, under the influence of competition, (competition itself being governed by certain laws, which laws are therefore the ultimate regulators of the division of the produce;) and employing certain expedients (as money, credit, etc.) to facilitate the distribution. All these operations, though many of them are really the result of a plurality of motives, are considered by political economy as flowing solely from the desire of wealth. The science then proceeds to investigate the laws which govern these several operations, under the supposition that man is a being who is determined, by the necessity of his nature, to prefer a greater portion of wealth to a small in all cases, without any other exception than that constituted by the two counter-motives already specified; not that any political economist was ever so absurd as to suppose that mankind are really thus constituted, but because this is the mode in which science must necessarily proceed. When an effect depends on a concurrence of causes, these causes must be studied one at a time, and their laws separately investigated, if we wish, through the causes, to obtain the power of either predicting or controlling the effect; since the law of the effect is compounded of the laws of all the causes which determine it. The law of the centripetal and that of the projectile force must have been known before the motions of the earth and planets could be explained or many of them predicted. The same is the case with the conduct of man in society. In order to judge how he will act under the variety of desires and aversions which are concurrently operating upon him, we must know how he would act under the exclusive influence of each one in particular. There is, perhaps, no action of a man's life in which he is neither under the immediate nor under the remote influence of any impulse but the mere desire of wealth. With respect to those parts of human conduct of which wealth is not even the principal object, to these political economy does not pretend that its conclusions are applicable. But there are also certain departments of human affairs in which the acquisition of wealth is the main and acknowledged end. It is only of these that political economy takes notice. The manner in which it necessarily proceeds is that of treating the main and acknowledged end as if it were the sole end; which, of all hypotheses equally simple, is the nearest to the truth. The political economist inquires, what are the actions which would be produced by this desire, if within the departments in question it were unimpeded by any other. In this way a nearer approximation is obtained than would otherwise be practicable to the real order of human affairs in those departments. This approximation has then to be corrected by making proper allowance for the effects of any impulses of a different description which can be shown to interfere with the result in any particular case. Only in a few of the most striking cases (such as the important one of the principle of population) are these corrections interpolated into the expositions of political economy itself; the strictness of purely scientific arrangement being thereby somewhat departed from, for the sake of practical utility. So far as it is known, or may be presumed, that the conduct of mankind in the pursuit of wealth is under the collateral influence of any other of the properties of our nature than the desire of obtaining the greatest quantity of wealth with the least labour and self-denial, the conclusions of political economy will so far fail of being applicable to the explanation or prediction of real events, until they are modified by a correct allowance for the degree of influence exercised by the other cause.'*

Extensive and important practical guidance may be derived, in any given state of society, from general propositions such as those above indicated; even though the modifying influence of the miscellaneous causes which the theory does not take into account, as well as the

* *Essays on some Unsettled Questions of Political Economy*, pp. 137-41.

effect of the general social changes in progress, be provisionally overlooked. And though it has been a very common error of political economists to draw conclusions from the elements of one state of society, and apply them to other states in which many of the elements are not the same, it is even then not difficult, by tracing back the demonstrations, and introducing the new premises in their proper places, to make the same general course of argument which served for the one case serve for the others too.

For example, it has been greatly the custom of English political economists to discuss the laws of the distribution of the produce of industry, on a supposition which is scarcely realised anywhere out of England and Scotland, namely, that the produce is 'shared among three classes, altogether distinct from one another, labourers, capitalists, and landlords; and that all these are free agents, permitted in law and in fact to set upon their labour, their capital, and their land, whatever price they are able to get for it. The conclusions of the science, being all adapted to a society thus constituted, require to be revised whenever they are applied to any other. They are inapplicable where the only capitalists are the landlords, and the labourers are their property, as in slave countries. They are inapplicable where the almost universal landlord is the State, as in India. They are inapplicable where the agricultural labourer is generally the owner both of the land itself and of the capital, as frequently in France, or of the capital only, as in Ireland.' But though it may often be very justly objected to the existing race of political economists 'that they attempt to construct a permanent fabric out of transitory materials; that they take for granted the immutability of arrangements of society, many of which are in their nature fluctuating or progressive, and enunciate, with as little qualification as if they were universal and absolute truths, propositions which are perhaps applicable to no state of society except the particular one in which the writer happened to live'; this does not take away the value of the propositions, considered with reference to the state of society from which they were drawn. And even as applicable to other states of society, 'it must not be supposed that the science is so incomplete and unsatisfactory as this might seem to prove. Though many of its conclusions are only locally true, its method of investigation is applicable universally; and as whoever has solved a certain number of algebraic equations can without difficulty solve all others of the same kind, so whoever knows the political economy of England, or even of Yorkshire, knows that of all nations, actual or possible, provided he have good sense enough not to expect the same conclusion to issue from varying premises.' Whoever has mastered with the degree of precision which is attainable the laws which, under free competition, determine the rent, profits, and wages, received by landlords, capitalists, and labourers, in a state of society in which the three classes are completely separate, will have no difficulty in determining the very different laws which regulate the distribution of the produce among the classes interested in it in any of the states of cultivation and landed property set forth in the foregoing extract.*

4. *Political ethology, or the science of national character*

I would not here undertake to decide what other hypothetical or abstract sciences similar to Political Economy may admit of being carved out of the general body of the social science; what other portions of the social phenomena are in a sufficiently close and complete dependence, in the first resort, on a peculiar class of causes, to make it convenient to create a preliminary science of those causes: postponing the consideration of the causes which act through them, or in concurrence with them, to a later period of the inquiry. There is, however, among these separate departments one which cannot be passed over in silence, being of a more comprehensive and commanding character than any of the other branches into which the social science may admit of being divided. Like them, it is directly conversant with the causes of only one class of social facts, but a class which exercises, immediately or remotely, a paramount influence over the rest. I allude to what may be termed Political Ethology, or the theory of the causes which determine the type of character belonging to a people or to an age. Of all the subordinate branches of the social science, this is the most completely in its infancy. The causes of national character are scarcely at all understood, and the effect of institutions or social arrangements upon the character of the people is generally that portion of their effects which is least attended to, and least

* The quotations in this paragraph are from a paper written by the author, and published in a periodical in 1834.

comprehended. Nor is this wonderful when we consider the infant state of the Science of Ethology itself, from whence the laws must be drawn, of which the truths of political ethology can be but results and exemplifications.

Yet to whoever well considers the matter, it must appear that the laws of national (or collective) character are by far the most important class of sociological laws. In the first place, the character which is formed by any state of social circumstances is in itself the most interesting phenomenon which that state of society can possibly present. Secondly, it is also a fact which enters largely into the production of all the other phenomena. And above all, the character, that is, the opinions, feelings, and habits of the people, though greatly the results of the state of society which precedes them, are also greatly the causes of the state of society which follows them; and are the power by which all those of the circumstances of society which are artificial – laws and customs, for instance – are altogether moulded: customs evidently, laws no less really, either by the direct influence of public sentiment upon the ruling powers, or by the effect which the state of national opinion and feeling has in determining the form of government, and shaping the character of the governors.

As might be expected, the most imperfect part of those branches of social inquiry which have been cultivated as separate sciences is the theory of the manner in which their conclusions are affected by ethological considerations. The omission is no defect in them as abstract or hypothetical sciences, but it vitiates them in their practical application as branches of a comprehensive social science. In political economy, for instance, empirical laws of human nature are tacitly assumed by English thinkers, which are calculated only for Great Britain and the United States. Among other things, an intensity of competition is constantly supposed, which, as a general mercantile fact, exists in no country in the world except these two. An English political economist, like his countrymen in general, has seldom learned that it is possible that men, in conducting the business of selling their goods over a counter, should care more about their ease or their vanity than about their pecuniary gain. Yet those who know the habits of the Continent of Europe are aware how apparently small a motive often outweighs the desire of money-getting, even in the operations which have money-getting for their direct object. The more highly the science of ethology is cultivated, and the better the diversities of individual and national character are understood, the smaller, probably, will the number of propositions become which it will be considered safe to build on as universal principles of human nature.

These considerations show that the process of dividing off the social science into compartments, in order that each may be studied separately, and its conclusions afterwards corrected for practice by the modifications supplied by the others, must be subject to at least one important limitation. Those portions alone of the social phenomena can with advantage be made the subjects, even provisionally, of distinct branches of science, into which the diversities of character between different nations or different times enter as influencing causes only in a secondary degree. Those phenomena, on the contrary, with which the influences of the ethological state of the people are mixed up at every step (so that the connection of effects and causes cannot be even rudely marked out without taking those influences into consideration) could not with any advantage, nor without great disadvantage, be treated independently of political ethology, nor, therefore, of all the circumstances by which the qualities of a people are influenced. For this reason (as well as for others which will hereafter appear) there can be no separate Science of Government; that being the fact which, of all others, is most mixed up, both as cause and effect, with the qualities of the particular people or of the particular age. All questions respecting the tendencies of forms of government must stand part of the general science of society, not of any separate branch of it.

This general Science of Society, as distinguished from the separate departments of the science (each of which asserts its conclusions only conditionally, subject to the paramount control of the laws of the general science) now remains to be characterised. And, as will be shown presently, nothing of a really scientific character is here possible, except by the inverse deductive method. But before we quit the subject of those sociological speculations which proceed by way of direct deduction, we must examine in what relation they stand to that indispensable element in all deductive sciences, Verification by Specific Experience – comparison between the conclusions of reasoning and the results of observation.

5. The empirical laws of the social science

We have seen that, in most deductive sciences, and among the rest in
Ethology itself, which is the immediate foundation of the Social
Science, a preliminary work of preparation is performed on the
observed facts, to fit them for being rapidly and accurately collated
(sometimes even for being collated at all) with the conclusions of
theory. This preparatory treatment consists in finding general
propositions which express concisely what is common to large classes
of observed facts; and these are called the empirical laws of the
phenomena. We have, therefore, to inquire, whether any similar
preparatory process can be performed on the facts of the social
science; whether there are any empirical laws in history or statistics.

In statistics it is evident that empirical laws may sometimes be
traced, and the tracing them forms an important part of that system
of indirect observation on which we must often rely for the data of
the Deductive Science. The process of the science consists in
inferring effects from their causes; but we have often no means of
observing the causes except through the medium of their effects. In
such cases the deductive science is unable to predict the effects, for
want of the necessary data; it can determine what causes are capable
of producing any given effect, but not with what frequency and in
what quantities those causes exist. An instance in point is afforded
by a newspaper now lying before me. A statement was furnished by
one of the official assignees in bankruptcy, showing, among the
various bankruptcies which it had been his duty to investigate, in
how many cases the losses had been caused by misconduct of
different kinds, and in how many by unavoidable misfortunes. The
result was, that the number of failures caused by misconduct greatly
preponderated over those arising from all other causes whatever.
Nothing but specific experience could have given sufficient ground for
a conclusion to this purport. To collect, therefore, such empirical laws
(which are never more than approximate generalisations) from direct
observation, is an important part of the process of sociological
inquiry.

The experimental process is not here to be regarded as a distinct
road to the truth, but as a means (happening accidentally to be the
only, or the best, available) for obtaining the necessary data for the
deductive science. When the immediate causes of social facts are not

open to direct observation, the empirical law of the effects gives us the empirical law (which in that case is all that we can obtain) of the causes likewise. But those immediate causes depend on remote causes; and the empirical law, obtained by this indirect mode of observation can only be relied on as applicable to unobserved cases, so long as there is reason to think that no change has taken place in any of the remote causes on which the immediate causes depend. In making use, therefore, of even the best statistical generalisations for the purpose of inferring (though it be only conjecturally) that the same empirical laws will hold in any new case, it is necessary that we be well acquainted with the remoter causes, in order that we may avoid applying the empirical law to cases which differ in any of the circumstances on which the truth of the law ultimately depends. And thus, even where conclusions derived from specific observation are available for practical inferences in new cases, it is necessary that the deductive science should stand sentinel over the whole process; that it should be constantly referred to, and its sanction obtained to every inference.

The same thing holds true of all generalisations which can be grounded on history. Not only are there such generalisations, but it will presently be shown that the general science of society, which inquires into the laws of succession and co-existence of the great facts constituting the state of society and civilisation at any time, can proceed in no other manner than by making such generalisations – afterwards to be confirmed by connecting them with the psychological and ethological laws on which they must really depend.

6. The verification of the social science

But (reserving this question for its proper place) in those more special inquiries which form the subject of the separate branches of the social science, this twofold logical process and reciprocal verification is not possible: specific experience affords nothing amounting to empirical laws. This is particularly the case where the object is to determine the effect of any one social cause among a great number acting simultaneously; the effect, for example, of corn laws, or of a prohibitive commercial system generally. Though it may be perfectly certain, from theory, what *kind* of effects corn laws must produce, and in what general direction their influence must tell upon industrial prosperity, their effect is yet of necessity so much disguised by the similar or contrary effects of other influencing agents, that specific experience can at most only show that on the average of some great number of instances, the cases where there were corn laws exhibited the effect in a greater degree than those where there were not. Now the number of instances necessary to exhaust the whole round of combinations of the various influential circumstances, and thus afford a fair average, never can be obtained. Not only we can never learn with sufficient authenticity the facts of so many instances, but the world itself does not afford them in sufficient numbers, within the limits of the given state of society and civilisation which such inquiries always presuppose. Having thus no previous empirical generalisations with which to collate the conclusions of theory, the only mode of direct verification which remains is to compare those conclusions with the result of an individual experiment or instance. But here the difficulty is equally great. For in order to verify a theory by an experiment, the circumstances of the experiment must be exactly the same with those contemplated in the theory. But in social phenomena the circumstances of no two cases are exactly alike. A trial of corn laws in another country or in a former generation would go a very little way towards verifiying a conclusion drawn respecting their effect in this generation and in this country. It thus happens, in most cases, that the only individual instance really fitted to verify the predictions of theory is the very instance for which the predictions were made; and the verification comes too late to be of any avail for practical guidance.

Although, however, direct verification is impossible, there is an indirect verification, which is scarcely of less value, and which is always practicable. The conclusion drawn as to the individual case can only be directly verified in that case; but it is verified indirectly by the verification of other conclusions, drawn in other individual cases from the same laws. The experience which comes too late to verify the particular proposition to which it refers is not too late to help towards verifying the general sufficiency of the theory. The test of the degree in which the science affords safe ground for predicting (and consequently for practically dealing with) what has not yet happened, is the degree in which it would have enabled us to predict what has actually occurred. Before our theory of the influence of a particular cause, in a given state of circumstances, can be entirely trusted, we must be able to explain and account for the existing state of all that portion of the social phenomena which that cause has a tendency to influence. If, for instance, we would apply our speculations in political economy to the prediction or guidance of the phenomena of any country, we must be able to explain all the mercantile or industrial facts of a general character appertaining to the present state of that country: to point out causes sufficient to account for all of them, and prove, or show good ground for supposing, that these causes have really existed. If we cannot do this, it is a proof either that the facts which ought to be taken into account are not yet completely known to us, or that although we know the facts, we are not masters of a sufficiently perfect theory to enable us to assign their consequences. In either case we are not, in the present state of our knowledge, fully competent to draw conclusions, speculative or practical, for that country. In like manner, if we would attempt to judge of the effect which any political institution would have, supposing that it could be introduced into any given country, we must be able to show that the existing state of the practical government of that country, and of whatever else depends thereon, together with the particular character and tendencies of the people, and their state in respect to the various elements of social well being, are such as the institutions they have lived under, in conjunction with the other circumstances of their nature or of their position, were calculated to produce.

To prove (in short) that our science, and our knowledge of the particular case, render us competent to predict the future, we must show that they would have enabled us to predict the present and the past. If there be anything which we could not have predicted, this constitutes a residual phenomenon, requiring further study for the purposes of explanation; and we must either search among the circumstances of the particular case until we find one which, on the principles of our existing theory, accounts for the unexplained phenomenon, or we must turn back, and seek the explanation by an extension and improvement of the theory itself.

CHAPTER TEN

Of the Inverse Deductive, or Historical Method

1. *Distinction between the general science of society and special sociological inquiries*

There are two kinds of sociological inquiry. In the first kind, the question proposed is, what effect will follow from a given cause, a certain general condition of social circumstances being presupposed. As, for example, what would be the effect of imposing or of repealing corn laws, of abolishing monarchy or introducing universal suffrage, in the present condition of society and civilisation in any European country, or under any other given supposition with regard to the circumstances of society in general, without reference to the changes which might take place, or which may already be in progress, in those circumstances. But there is also a second inquiry, namely, what are the laws which determine those general circumstances themselves. In this last the question is, not what will be the effect of a given cause in a certain state of society, but what are the causes which produce, and the phenomena which characterise, States of Society generally. In the solution of this question consists the general Science of Society, by which the conclusions of the other and more special kind of inquiry must be limited and controlled.

2. *What is meant by a state of society?*

In order to conceive correctly the scope of this general science, and distinguish it from the subordinate departments of sociological speculation, it is necessary to fix the ideas attached to the phrase 'a State of Society'. What is called a state of society is the simultaneous state of all the greater social facts or phenomena. Such are the degree of knowledge, and of intellectual and moral culture, existing in the community, and of every class of it; the state of industry, of wealth and its distribution; the habitual occupations of the community; their division into classes, and the relations of those classes to one another; the common beliefs which they entertain on all the subjects most important to mankind, and the degree of assurance with which those beliefs are held; their tastes, and the character and degree of their aesthetic development; their form of government, and the more important of their laws and customs. The condition of all these things, and of many more which will readily suggest themselves, constitute the state of society or the state of civilisation at any given time.

When states of society, and the causes which produce them, are spoken of as a subject of science, it is implied that there exists a natural correlation among these different elements; that not every variety of combination of these general social facts is possible, but only certain combinations; that, in short, there exist Uniformities of Co-existence between the states of the various social phenomena. And such is the truth; as is indeed a necessary consequence of the influence exercised by every one of those phenomena over every other. It is a fact implied in the *consensus* of the various parts of the social body.

States of society are like different constitutions or different ages in the physical frame; they are conditions not of one or a few organs or functions, but of the whole organism. Accordingly, the information which we possess respecting past ages, and respecting the various states of society now existing in different regions of the earth, does, when duly analysed, exhibit uniformities. It is found that when one of the features of society is in a particular state, a state of many other features, more or less precisely determinate, always or usually co-exists with it.

But the uniformities of co-existence obtaining among phenomena which are effects of causes must (as we have so often observed) be corollaries from the laws of causation by which these phenomena are really determined. The mutual correlation between the different elements of each state of society is therefore a derivative law, resulting from the laws which regulate the succession between one state of society and another; for the proximate cause of every state of society is the state of society immediately preceding it. The fundamental problem, therefore, of the social science, is to find the laws according to which any state of society produces the state which succeeds it and takes its place. This opens the great and vexed question of the progressiveness of man and society; an idea involved in every just conception of social phenomena as the subject of a science.

3. The progressiveness of man and society

It is one of the characters, not absolutely peculiar to the sciences of human nature and society, but belonging to them in a peculiar degree, to be conversant with a subject-matter whose properties are changeable. I do not mean changeable from day to day, but from age to age; so that not only the qualities of individuals vary, but those of the majority are not the same in one age as in another.

The principal cause of this peculiarity is the extensive and constant reaction of the effects upon their causes. The circumstances in which mankind are placed, operating according to their own laws and to the laws of human nature, form the characters of the human beings; but the human beings, in their turn, mould and shape the circumstances for themselves and for those who come after them. From this reciprocal action there must necessarily result either a cycle or a progress. In astronomy also, every fact is at once effect and cause; the successive positions of the various heavenly bodies produce changes both in the direction and in the intensity of the forces by which those positions are determined. But in the case of the solar system, these mutual actions bring round again, after a certain number of changes, the former state of circumstances; which of course leads to the perpetual recurrence of the same series in an unvarying order. Those bodies, in short, revolve in orbits: but there are (or, conformably to the laws of astronomy, there might be) others which, instead of an orbit, describe a trajectory – a course not returning into itself. One or other of these must be the type to which human affairs must conform.

One of the thinkers who earliest conceived the succession of historical events as subject to fixed laws, and endeavoured to discover these laws by an analytical survey of history, Vico, the celebrated author of *Scienza Nuova*, adopted the former of these opinions. He conceived the phenomena of human society as revolving in an orbit; as going through periodically the same series of changes. Though there were not wanting circumstances tending to give some plausibility to this view, it would not bear a close scrutiny; and those who have succeeded Vico in this kind of speculations have universally adopted the idea of a trajectory or progress, in lieu of an orbit or cycle.

The words Progress and Progressiveness are not here to be understood as synonymous with improvement and tendency to improvement. It is conceivable that the laws of human nature might determine, and even necessitate, a certain series of changes in man and society, which might not in every case, or which might not on the whole, be improvements. It is my belief indeed that the general tendency is, and will continue to be, saving occasional and temporary exceptions, one of improvement – a tendency towards a better and happier state. This, however, is not a question of the method of the social science, but a theorem of the science itself. For our purpose it is sufficient that there is a progressive change, both in the character of the human race and in their outward circumstances so far as moulded by themselves; that in each successive age the principal phenomena of society are different from what they were in the age preceding, and still more different from any previous age: the periods which most distinctly mark these successive changes being intervals of one generation, during which a new set of human beings have been educated, have grown up from childhood, and taken possession of society.

The progressiveness of the human race is the foundation on which a method of philosophising in the social science has been of late years erected, far superior to either of the two modes which had previously been prevalent, the chemical or experimental, and the geometrical modes. This method, which is now generally adopted by the most advanced thinkers on the Continent, consists in attempting, by a study and analysis of the general facts of history, to discover (what these philosophers term) the law of progress; which law, once ascertained, must according to them enable us to predict future events, just as after a few terms of an infinite series in algebra we are able to detect the principle of regularity in their formation, and to predict the rest of the series to any number of terms we please. The principal aim of historical speculation in France, of late years, has been to ascertain this law. But while I gladly acknowledge the great services which have been rendered to historical knowledge by this school, I cannot but deem them to be mostly chargeable with a fundamental misconception of the true method of social philosophy. The misconception consists in supposing that the order of succession which we may be able to trace among the different states of society and civilisation which history presents to us, even if that order were more rigidly uniform than it has yet been proved to be, could ever amount to a law of nature. It can only be an empirical law. The succession of states of the human mind and of human society cannot have an independent law of its own; it must depend on the psychological and ethological laws which govern the action of circumstances on men and of men on circumstances. It is conceivable that those laws might be such, and the general circumstances of the human race such, as to determine the successive transformations of man and society to one given and unvarying order. But even if the case were so, it cannot be the ultimate aim of science to discover an empirical law. Until that law could be connected with the psychological and ethological laws on which it must depend, and, by the consilience of deduction *à priori* with historical evidence, could be converted from an empirical law into a scientific one, it could not be relied on for the prediction of future events, beyond, at most, strictly adjacent cases. M. Comte alone, among the new historical school, has seen the necessity of thus connecting all our generalisations from history with the laws of human nature.

4. *The laws of the succession of states of society can only be ascertained by the inverse deductive method*

But while it is an imperative rule never to introduce any generalisation from history into the social science unless sufficient grounds can be pointed out for it in human nature, I do not think any one will contend that it would have been possible, setting out from the principles of human nature and from the general circumstances of the position of our species to determine *à priori* the order in which human development must take place, and to predict, consequently, the general facts of history up to the present time. After the first few terms of the series, the influence exercised over each generation by the generations which preceded it becomes (as is well observed by the writer last referred to) more and more preponderant over all other influences; until at length what we now are and do is in a very small degree the result of the universal circumstances of the human race, or even of our own circumstances acting through the original qualities of our species, but mainly of the qualities produced in us by the whole previous history of humanity. So long a series of actions and reactions between Circumstances and Man, each successive term being composed of an ever greater number and variety of parts, could not possibly be computed by human faculties from the elementary laws which produce it. The mere length of the series would be a sufficient obstacle, since a slight error in any one of the terms would augment in rapid progression at every subsequent step.

If, therefore, the series of the effects themselves did not, when examined as a whole, manifest any regularity, we should in vain attempt to construct a general science of society. We must in that case have contented ourselves with that subordinate order of sociological speculation formerly noticed, namely, with endeavouring to ascertain what would be the effect of the introduction of any new cause, in a state of society supposed to be fixed; a knowledge sufficient for the more common exigencies of daily political practice, but liable to fail in all cases in which the progressive movement of society is one of the influencing elements; and therefore more precarious in proportion as the case is more important. But since both the natural varieties of mankind, and the original diversities of local circumstances are much less considerable than the points of agreement, there will naturally be a certain degree of uniformity in the progressive development of the species and of its works. And this uniformity tends to become greater, not less, as society advances; since the evolution of each people, which is at first determined exclusively by the nature and circumstances of that people, is gradually brought under the influence (which becomes stronger as civilisation advances) of the other nations of the earth, and of the circumstances by which they have been influenced. History accordingly does, when judiciously examined, afford Empirical Laws of Society. And the problem of general sociology is to ascertain these, and connect them with the laws of human nature, by deductions showing that such were the derivative laws naturally to be expected as the consequences of those ultimate ones.

It is, indeed, hardly ever possible, even after history has suggested the derivative law, to demonstrate *à priori* that such was the only order of succession or of co-existence in which the effects could, consistently with the laws of human nature, have been produced. We can at most make out that there were strong *à priori* reasons for expecting it, and that no other order of succession or co-existence would have been so likely to result from the nature of man and the general circumstances of his position. Often we cannot do even this; we cannot even show that what did take place was probable *à priori*, but only that it was possible. This, however, – which, in the Inverse Deductive Method, that we are now characterising, is a real process of verification, – is as indispensable as verification by specific experience has been shown to be, where the conclusion is originally obtained by the direct way of deduction. The empirical laws must be the result of but a few instances, since few nations have ever attained at all, and still fewer by their own independent development, a high stage of social progress. If, therefore, even one or two of these few instances be insufficiently known, or imperfectly analysed into their elements, and therefore not adequately compared with other instances, nothing is more probable than that a wrong empirical law will emerge instead of the right one. Accordingly, the most erroneous generalisations are continually made from the course of history: not only in this country, where history cannot yet be said to be at all cultivated as a science, but in other countries where it is so cultivated, and by persons well versed in it. The only check or corrective is constant verification by psychological and ethological laws. We may add to this, that no one but a person competently skilled in those laws is capable of preparing the materials for historical generalisation by analysing the facts of history, or even by observing the social phenomena of his own time. No other will be aware of the comparative importance of different facts, nor consequently know what facts to look for or to observe; still less will he be capable of estimating the evidence of facts which, as is the case with most, cannot be ascertained by direct observation or learnt from testimony, but must be inferred from marks.

5. Social statics, or the science of the co-existences of social phenomena

The Empirical Laws of Society are of two kinds; some are uniformities of co-existence, some of succession. According as the science is occupied in ascertaining and verifying the former sort of uniformities or the latter, M. Comte gives it the title of Social Statics or of Social Dynamics, comformably to the distinction in mechanics between the conditions of equilibrium and those of movement, or in biology between the laws of organisation and those of life. The first branch of the science ascertains the conditions of stability in the social union; the second, the laws of progress. Social Dynamics is the theory of society considered in a state of progressive movement: while Social Statics is the theory of the *consensus* already spoken of as existing among the different parts of the social organism; in other words, the theory of the mutual actions and reactions of contemporaneous social phenomena –

> making* provisionally, as far as possible, abstraction, for scientific purposes, of the fundamental movement which is at all times gradually modifying the whole of them.
>
> In this first point of view, the provisions of sociology will enable us to infer one from another (subject to ulterior verification by direct observation) the various characteristic marks of each distinct mode of social existence; in a manner essentially analogous to what is now habitually practised in the anatomy of the physical body. This preliminary aspect, therefore, of political science, of necessity supposes that (contrary to the existing habits of philosophers) each of the numerous elements of the social state, ceasing to be looked at independently and absolutely, shall be always and exclusively considered relatively to all the other elements, with the whole of which it is united by mutual interdependence. It would be superfluous to insist here upon the great and constant utility of this branch of sociological speculation. It is, in the first place, the indispensable basis of the theory of social progress. It may, moreover, be employed, immediately and of itself, to supply the place, provisionally at least, of direct observation, which in many cases is not always practicable for some of the elements of society, the real condition of which may, however, be sufficiently judged of by means of the relations which connect them with others previously known. The history of the science may give us some notion of the habitual importance of this auxiliary resource, by reminding us, for example, how the vulgar errors of mere erudition concerning the pretended acquirements of the ancient Egyptians in the higher astronomy, were irrevocably dissipated (even before sentence had been passed on them by a sounder erudition) from the single consideration of the inevitable connection between the general state of astronomy and that of abstract geometry, then evidently in its infancy. It would be easy to cite a multitude of

---

* Auguste Comte, *Cours de Philosophie Positive* iv. 325-9.

analogous cases, the character of which could admit of no dispute. In order to avoid exaggeration, however, it should be remarked that these necessary relations among the different aspects of society cannot, from their very nature, be so simple and precise that the results observed could only have arisen from some one mode of mutual co-ordination. Such a notion, already too narrow in the science of life, would be completely at variance with the still more complex nature of sociological speculations. But the exact estimation of these limits of variation, both in the healthy and in the morbid state, constitutes, at least as much as in the anatomy of the natural body, an indispensable complement to every theory of Sociological Statics, without which the indirect exploration above spoken of would often lead into error.

This is not the place for methodically demonstrating the existence of a necessary relation among all the possible aspects of the same social organism; a point on which, in principle at least, there is now little difference of opinion among sound thinkers. From whichever of the social elements we choose to set out, we may easily recognise that it has always a connection, more or less immediate, with all the other elements, even with those which at first sight appear the most independent of it. The dynamical consideration of the progressive development of civilised humanity, affords, no doubt, a still more efficacious means of effecting this interesting verification of the *consensus* of the social phenomena, by displaying the manner in which every change in any one part operates immediately, or very speedily, upon all the rest. But this indication may be preceded, or at all events followed, by a confirmation of a purely statical kind; for, in politics as in mechanics, the communication of motion from one object to another proves a connection between them. Without descending to the minute interdependence of the different branches of any one science or art, is it not evident that among the different sciences, as well as among most of the arts, there exists such a connection, that if the state of any one well-marked division of them is sufficiently known to us, we can with real scientific assurance infer, from their necessary correlation, the contemporaneous state of every one of the others? By a further extension of this consideration, we may conceive the necessary relation which exists between the condition of the sciences in general and that of the arts in general, except that the mutual dependence is less intense in proportion as it is more indirect. The same is the case when, instead of considering the aggregate of the social phenomena in some one people, we examine it simultaneously in different contemporaneous nations, between which the perpetual reciprocity of influence, especially in modern times, cannot be contested, though the *consensus* must in this case be ordinarily of a less decided character, and must decrease gradually with the affinity of the cases and the multiplicity of the points of contact, so as at last, in some cases, to disappear almost entirely; as, for example, between Western Europe and Eastern Asia, of which the various general states of society appear to have been hitherto almost independent of one another.

These remarks are followed by illustrations of one of the most important, and, until lately, most neglected, of the general principles which, in this division of the social science, may be considered as established; namely, the necessary correlation between the form of government existing in any society and the contemporaneous state of civilisation: a natural law which stamps the endless discussions and innumerable theories respecting forms of government in the abstract as fruitless and worthless for any other purpose than as a preparatory treatment of materials to be afterwards used for the construction of a better philosophy.

As already remarked, one of the main results of the science of social statics would be to ascertain the requisites of stable political union. There are some circumstances which, being found in all societies without exception, and in the greatest degree where the social union is most complete, may be considered (when psychological and ethological laws confirm the indication) as conditions of the existence of the complex phenomenon called a State. For example, no numerous society has ever been held together without laws, or usages equivalent to them; without tribunals, and an organised force of some sort to execute their decisions. There have always been public authorities whom, with more or less strictness, and in cases more or less accurately defined, the rest of the community obeyed, or according to general opinion were bound to obey. By following out this course of inquiry we shall find a number of requisites which have been present in every society that has maintained a collective existence, and on the cessation of which it has either merged in some other society, or reconstructed itself on some new basis, in which the conditions were conformed to. Although these results, obtained by comparing different forms and states of society, amount in themselves only to empirical laws, some of them, when once suggested, are found to follow with so much probability from general laws of human nature, that the consilience of the two processes raises the evidence to proof, and the generalisations to the rank of scientific truths.

This seems to be affirmable (for instance) of the conclusions arrived at in the following passage, extracted, with some alterations, from a criticism on the negative philosophy of the eighteenth century,* and which I quote, though (as in some former instances) from myself, because I have no better way of illustrating the conception I have formed of the kind of theorems of which sociological statics would consist:

The very first element of the social union, obedience to a government of some sort, has not been found so easy a thing to establish in the world. Among a timid and spiritless race like the inhabitants of the vast plains of tropical countries, passive obedience may be of natural growth; though even there we doubt whether it has ever been found among any people with whom fatalism, or, in other words, submission to the pressure of circumstances as a divine decree, did not prevail as a religious doctrine. But the difficulty of inducing a brave and warlike race to submit their individual *arbitrium* to any common umpire has always been felt to be so great, that nothing short of supernatural power has been deemed adequate to overcome it; and such tribes have always assigned to the first institution of civil society a divine origin. So differently did those judge who knew savage men by actual experience, from those who had no acquaintance with them except in the civilised state. In modern Europe itself, after the fall of the Roman Empire, to subdue the feudal anarchy and bring the whole people of any European nation into subjection to government (though Christianity in the most concentrated form of its influence was co-operating in the work) required thrice as many centuries as have elapsed since that time.

Now if these philosophers had known human nature under any other type than that of their own age, and of the particular classes of society among whom they lived, it would have occurred to them, that wherever this habitual submission to law and government has been firmly and durably established, and yet the vigour and manliness of character which resisted its establishment have been in any degree preserved, certain requisites have existed, certain conditions have been fulfilled, of which the following may be regarded as the principal:

First, there has existed, for all who were accounted citizens, – for all who were not slaves, kept down by brute force, – a system of *education*, beginning with infancy and continued through life, of which, whatever else it might include, one main and incessant ingredient was *restraining discipline*. To train the human being in the habit, and thence the power, of subordinating his personal impulses and aims to what were considered the ends of society; of adhering, against all temptation, to the course of conduct which those ends prescribed; of controlling in himself all feelings which were liable to militate against

* Since reprinted entire in *Dissertations and Discussions*, as the concluding paper of the first volume.

those ends, and encouraging all such as tended towards them; this was the purpose to which every outward motive that the authority directing the system could command, and every inward power or principle which its knowledge of human nature enabled it to evoke, were endeavoured to be rendered instrumental. The entire civil and military policy of the ancient commonwealths was such a system of training; in modern nations its place has been attempted to be supplied, principally, by religious teaching. And whenever and in proportion as the strictness of the restraining discipline was relaxed, the natural tendency of mankind to anarchy reasserted itself; the state became disorganised from within; mutual conflict for selfish ends neutralised the energies which were required to keep up the contest against natural causes of evil; and the nation, after a longer or briefer interval of progressive decline, became either the slave of a despotism, or the prey of a foreign invader.

The second condition of permanent political society has been found to be the existence, in some form or other, of the feeling of allegiance or loyalty. This feeling may vary in its objects, and is not confined to any particular form of government; but whether in a democracy or in a monarchy, its essence is always the same, viz. that there be in the constitution of the state *something* which is settled, something permanent, and not to be called in question; something which, by general agreement, has a right to be where it is, and to be secure against disturbance, whatever else may change. This feeling may attach itself, as among the Jews, (and in most of the commonwealths of antiquity,) to a common God or gods, the protectors and guardians of their state. Or it may attach itself to certain persons, who are deemed to be, whether by divine appointment, by long prescription, or by the general recognition of their superior capacity and worthiness, the rightful guides and guardians of the rest. Or it may connect itself with laws; with ancient liberties or ordinances. Or, finally, (and this is the only shape in which the feeling is likely to exist hereafter,) it may attach itself to the principles of individual freedom and political and social equality, as realised in institutions which as yet exist nowhere, or exist only in a rudimentary state. But in all political societies which have had a durable existence there has been some fixed point, something which people agree in holding sacred; which, wherever freedom of discussion was a recognised principle, it was of course lawful to contest in theory, but which no one could either fear or hope to see shaken in practice; which, in short (except perhaps during some temporary crisis) was in the common estimation placed beyond discussion. And the necessity of this may easily be made evident. A state never is, nor, until mankind are vastly improved, can hope to be, for any long time exempt from internal dissension; for there neither is nor ever has been any state of society in which collisions did not occur between the immediate interests and passions of powerful sections of the people. What, then, enables nations to weather these storms, and pass through turbulent times without any permanent weakening of the securities for peaceable existence? Precisely this – that however important the interests about which men fell out, the conflict did not affect the fundamental principle of the system of social union which happened to exist, nor threaten large portions of the community with the subversion of that on which they had built their calculations, and with which their hopes and aims had become identified. But when the questioning of these fundamental principles is (not the occasional disease or salutary medicine, but) the habitual condition of the body politic, and when all the violent animosities are called forth which spring naturally from such a situation, the state is virtually in a position of civil war, and can never long remain free from it in act and fact.

The third essential condition of stability in political society is a strong and active principle of cohesion among the members of the same community or state. We need scarcely say that we do not mean nationality, in the vulgar sense of the term; a senseless antipathy to foreigners; indifference to the general welfare of the human race, or an unjust preference of the supposed interest of our own country; a cherishing of bad peculiarities because they are national, or a refusal to adopt what has been found good by other countries. We mean a principle of sympathy, not of hostility; of union, not of separation. We mean a feeling of common interest among those who live under the same government, and are contained within the same natural or historical boundaries. We mean, that one part of the community do not consider themselves as foreigners with regard to another part; that they set a value on their connection – feel that they are one people, that their lot is cast together, that evil to any of their fellow-countrymen is evil to themselves, and do not desire selfishly to free themselves from their share of any common inconvenience by severing the connection. How strong this feeling was in those ancient commonwealths which attained any durable greatness every one knows. How happily Rome, in spite of all her tyranny, succeeded in establishing the feeling of a common country among the provinces of her vast and divided empire, will appear when any one who has given due attention to the subject shall take the trouble to point it out. In modern times the countries which have had that feeling in the strongest degree have been the most powerful countries; England, France, and, in proportion to their territory and resources, Holland and Switzerland; while England in her connection with Ireland is one of the most signal examples of the consequences of its absence. Every Italian knows why Italy is under a foreign yoke; every German knows what maintains despotism in the Austrian empire;* the evils of Spain flow as much from the absence of nationality among the Spaniards themselves as from the presence of it in their relations with foreigners: while the completest illustration of

* (Written and first published in 1840.)

all is afforded by the republics of South America, where the parts of one and the same state adhere so slightly together, that no sooner does any province think itself aggrieved by the general government than it proclaims itself a separate nation.

6. *Social dynamics, or the science of the successions of social phenomena*

While the derivative laws of social statics are ascertained by analysing different states of society, and comparing them with one another, without regard to the order of their succession, the consideration of the successive order is, on the contrary, predominant in the study of social dynamics, of which the aim is to observe and explain the sequences of social conditions. This branch of the social science would be as complete as it can be made if every one of the leading general circumstances of each generation were traced to its causes in the generation immediately preceding. But the *consensus* is so complete (especially in modern history) that, in the filiation of one generation and another, it is the whole which produces the whole, rather than any part a part. Little progress, therefore, can be made in establishing the filiation directly from laws of human nature, without having first ascertained the immediate or derivative laws according to which social states generate one another as society advances – the *axiomata media* of General Sociology.

The empirical laws which are most readily obtained by generalisation from history do not amount to this. They are not the 'middle principles' themselves, but only evidence towards the establishment of such principles. They consist of certain general tendencies which may be perceived in society; a progressive increase of some social elements and diminution of others, or a gradual change in the general character of certain elements. It is easily seen, for instance, that as society advances, mental tend more and more to prevail over bodily qualities, and masses over individuals; that the occupation of all that portion of mankind who are not under external restraint is at first chiefly military, but society becomes progressively more and more engrossed with productive pursuits, and the military spirit gradually gives way to the industrial; to which many similar truths might be added. And with generalisations of this description ordinary inquirers, even of the historical school now predominant on the Continent, are satisfied. But these and all such results are still at too great a distance from the elementary laws of human nature on which they depend, – too many links intervene, and the concurrence of causes at each link is far too complicated, – to enable these propositions to be presented as direct corollaries from those elementary principles. They have, therefore, in the minds of most inquirers, remained in the state of empirical laws, applicable only within the bounds of actual observation, without any means of determining their real limits, and of judging whether the changes which have hitherto been in progress are destined to continue indefinitely, or to terminate, or even to be reversed.

7. Outlines of the historical method

In order to obtain better empirical laws, we must not rest satisfied with noting the progressive changes which manifest themselves in the separate elements of society, and in which nothing is indicated but the relation of fragments of the effect to corresponding fragments of the cause. It is necessary to combine the statical view of social phenomena with the dynamical, considering not only the progressive changes of the different elements, but the contemporaneous condition of each, and thus obtain empirically the law of correspondence not only between the simultaneous states, but between the simultaneous changes, of those elements. This law of correspondence it is which, duly verified à priori, would become the real scientific derivative law of the development of humanity and human affairs.

In the difficult process of observation and comparison which is here required, it would evidently be a great assistance if it should happen to be the fact that some one element in the complex existence of social man is pre-eminent over all others as the prime agent of the social movement. For we could then take the progress of that one element as the central chain, to each successive link of which the corresponding links of all the other progressions being appended, the succession of the facts would by this alone be presented in a kind of spontaneous order, far more nearly approaching to the real order of their filiation than could be obtained by any other merely empirical process.

Now, the evidence of history and that of human nature combine, by a striking instance of consilience, to show that there really is one social element which is thus predominant, and almost paramount, among the agents of the social progression. This is the state of the speculative faculties of mankind, including the nature of the beliefs which by any means they have arrived at concerning themselves and the world by which they are surrounded.

It would be a great error, and one very little likely to be committed, to assert that speculation, intellectual activity, the pursuit of truth, is among the more powerful propensities of human nature, or holds a predominating place in the lives of any, save decidedly exceptional, individuals. But, notwithstanding the relative weakness of this principle among other sociological agents, its influence is the main determining cause of the social progress; all the other dispositions of our nature which contribute to that progress being dependent on it for the means of accomplishing their share of the work. Thus (to take the most obvious case first) the impelling force to most of the improvements effected in the arts of life is the desire of increased material comfort; but as we can only act upon external objects in proportion to our knowledge of them, the state of knowledge at any time is the limit of the industrial improvements possible at that time; and the progress of industry must follow, and depend on, the progress of knowledge. The same thing may be shown to be true, thought it is not quite so obvious, of the progress of the fine arts. Further, as the strongest propensities of uncultivated or half-cultivated human nature (being the purely selfish ones, and those of a sympathetic character which partake most of the nature of selfishness) evidently tend in themselves to disunite mankind, not to unite them, – to make them rivals, not confederates; social existence is only possible by a disciplining of those more powerful propensities, which consists in subordinating them to a common system of opinions. The degree of this subordination is the measure of the completeness of the social union, and the nature of the common opinions determines its kind. But in order that mankind should conform their actions to any set of opinions, these opinions must exist, must be believed by them. And thus the state of the speculative faculties, the character of the propositions assented to by the intellect, essentially determines the moral and political state of the community, as we have already seen that it determines the physical.

These conclusions, deduced from the laws of human nature, are in entire accordance with the general facts of history. Every considerable change historically known to us in the condition of any portion of mankind, when not brought about by external force, has been preceded by a change of proportional extent in the state of their knowledge or in their prevalent beliefs. As between any given state of speculation and the correlative state of everything else, it was almost always the former which first showed itself; though the effects, no doubt, reacted potently upon the cause. Every considerable advance in material civilisation has been preceded by an advance in knowledge; and when any great social change has come to pass, either in the way of gradual development or of sudden conflict, it has had for its precursor a great change in the opinions and modes of thinking of society. Polytheism, Judaism, Christianity, Protestantism, the critical philosophy of modern Europe, and its positive science – each of these has been a primary agent in making society what it was at each successive period, while society was but secondarily instrumental in making *them*, each of them (so far as causes can be assigned for its existence) being mainly an emanation not from the practical life of the period, but from the previous state of belief and thought. The weakness of the speculative propensity in mankind generally has not, therefore, prevented the progress of speculation from governing that of society at large; it has only, and too often, prevented progress altogether, where the intellectual progression has come to an early stand for want of sufficiently favourable circumstances.

From this accumulated evidence, we are justified in concluding that the order of human progression in all respects will mainly depend on the order of progression in the intellectual convictions of mankind, that is, on the law of the successive transformations of human opinions. The question remains, whether this law can be determined, at first from history as an empirical law, then converted into a scientific theorem by deducing it *à priori* from the principles of human nature. As the progress of knowledge and the changes in the opinions of mankind are very slow, and manifest themselves in a well-defined manner only at long intervals, it cannot be expected that the general order of sequence should be discoverable from the examination of less than a very considerable part of the duration of the social progress. It is necessary to take into consideration the whole of past time, from the first recorded condition of the human race, to the memorable phenomena of the last and present generations.

8. *Future prospects of sociological inquiry*

The investigation which I have thus endeavoured to characterise has been systematically attempted, up to the present time, by M. Comte alone. His work is hitherto the only known example of the study of social phenomena according to this conception of the Historical Method. Without discussing here the worth of his conclusions, and especially of his predictions and recommendations with respect to the Future of society, which appear to me greatly inferior in value to his appreciation of the Past, I shall confine myself to mentioning one important generalisation, which M. Comte regards as the fundamental law of the progress of human knowledge. Speculation he conceives to have, on every subject of human inquiry, three successive stages; in the first of which it tends to explain the phenomena by supernatural agencies, in the second by metaphysical abstractions, and in the third or final state confines itself to ascertaining their laws of succession and similitude. This generalisation appears to me to have that high degree of scientific evidence which is derived from the concurrence of the indications of history with the probabilities derived from the constitution of the human mind. Nor could it be easily conceived, from the mere enunciation of such a proposition, what a flood of light it lets in upon the whole course of history, when its consequences are traced, by connecting with each of the three states of human intellect which it distinguishes, and with each successive modification of those three states, the correlative condition of other social phenomena.*

* This great generalisation is often unfavourably criticised (as by Dr Whewell, for instance) under a misapprehension of its real import. The doctrine that the theological explanation of phenomena belongs only to the infancy of our knowledge of them, ought not to be construed as if it was equivalent to the assertion that mankind, as their knowledge advances, will necessarily cease to believe in any kind of theology. This was M. Comte's opinion; but it is by no means implied in his fundamental theorem. All that is implied is, that in an advanced state of human knowledge, no other Ruler of the World will be acknowledged than one who rules by universal laws, and does not at all, or does not unless in very peculiar cases, produce events by special interpositions. Originally all natural events were ascribed to such interpositions. At present every educated person rejects this explanation in regard to all classes of phenomena of which the laws have been fully ascertained; though some have not yet reached the point of referring all phenomena to the idea of Law, but believe that rain and sunshine, famine and pestilence, victory and defeat, death and life, are issues which the Creator does not leave to the operation of his general laws, but reserves to be decided by express acts of

But whatever decision competent judges may pronounce on the results arrived at by any individual inquirer, the method now characterised is that by which the derivative laws of social order and of social progress must be sought. By its aid we may hereafter succeed not only in looking far forward into the future history of the human race, but in determining what artificial means may be used, and to what extent, to accelerate the natural progress in so far as it is beneficial; to compensate for whatever may be its inherent inconveniences or disadvantages, and to guard against the dangers or accidents to which our species is exposed from the necessary incidents of its progression. Such practical instructions, founded on the highest branch of speculative sociology, will form the noblest and most beneficial portion of the Political Art.

That of this science and art even the foundations are but beginning to be laid is sufficiently evident. But the superior minds are fairly turning themselves towards that object. It has become the aim of really scientific thinkers to connect by theories the facts of universal history: it is acknowledged to be one of the requisites of a general system of social doctrine that it should explain, so far as the data exist, the main facts of history; and a Philosophy of History is generally admitted to be at once the verification and the initial form of the Philosophy of the Progress of Society.

---

volition. M. Comte's theory is the negation of this doctrine.

Dr Whewell equally misunderstands M. Comte's doctrine respecting the second or metaphysical stage of speculation. M. Comte did not mean that 'discussions concerning ideas' are limited to an early stage of inquiry, and cease when science enters into the positive stage. (*Philosophy of Discovery*, p. 226 et seq.) In all M. Comte's speculations as much stress is laid on the process of clearing up our conceptions as on the ascertainment of facts. When M. Comte speaks of the metaphysical stage of speculation, he means the stage in which men speak of 'Nature' and other abstractions as if they were active forces, producing effects; when Nature is said to do this, or forbid that; when Nature's horror of a vacuum, Nature's non-admission of a break, Nature's *vis medicatrix*, were offered as explanations of phenomena; when the qualities of things were mistaken for real entities dwelling in the things; when the phenomena of living bodies were thought to be accounted for by being referred to a 'vital force;' when, in short, the abstract names of phenomena were mistaken for the causes of their existence. In this sense of the word it cannot be reasonably denied that the metaphysical explanation of phenomena, equally with the theological, gives way before the advance of real science.

That the final, or positive stage, as conceived by M. Comte, has been equally misunderstood, and that, notwithstanding some expressions open to just criticism, M. Comte never dreamed of denying the legitimacy of inquiry into all causes which are accessible to human investigation, I have pointed out in a former place.

If the endeavours now making in all the more cultivated nations, and beginning to be made even in England, (usually the last to enter into the general movement of the European mind,) for the construction of a Philosophy of History, shall be directed and controlled by those views of the nature of sociological evidence which I have (very briefly and imperfectly) attempted to characterise, they cannot fail to give birth to a sociological system widely removed from the vague and conjectural character of all former attempts, and worthy to take its place, at last, among the sciences. When this time shall come, no important branch of human affairs will be any longer abandoned to empiricism and unscientific surmise; the circle of human knowledge will be complete, and it can only thereafter receive further enlargement by perpetual expansion from within.

CHAPTER ELEVEN

Additional Elucidations of the Science of History

1. *The subjection of historical facts to uniform laws is verified by statistics*

The doctrine which the preceding chapters were intended to enforce and elucidate – that the collective series of social phenomena, in other words, the course of history, is subject to general laws, which philosophy may possibly detect – has been familiar for generations to the scientific thinkers of the Continent, and has for the last quarter of a century passed out of their peculiar domain into that of newspapers and ordinary political discussion. In our own country, however, at the time of the first publication of this Treatise, it was almost a novelty, and the prevailing habits of thought on historical subjects were the very reverse of a preparation for it. Since then a great change has taken place, and has been eminently promoted by the important work of Mr Buckle, who, with characteristic energy, flung down this great principle, together with many striking exemplifications of it, into the arena of popular discussion, to be fought over by a sort of combatants in the presence of a sort of spectators, who would never even have been aware that there existed such a principle if they had been left to learn its existence from the speculations of pure science. And hence has arisen a considerable amount of controversy, tending not only to make the principle rapidly familiar to the majority of cultivated minds, but also to clear it from the confusions and misunderstandings by which it was but natural that it should for a time be clouded, and which impair the worth of the doctrine to those who accept it, and are the stumbling-block of many who do not.

Among the impediments to the general acknowledgment, by

thoughtful minds, of the subjection of historical facts to scientific laws, the most fundamental continues to be that which is grounded on the doctrine of Free Will, or, in other words, on the denial that the law of invariable Causation holds true of human volitions; for if it does not, the course of history, being the result of human volitions, cannot be a subject of scientific laws, since the volitions on which it depends can neither be foreseen nor reduced to any canon of regularity even after they have occurred. I have discussed this question, as far as seemed suitable to the occasion, in a former chapter, and I only think it necessary to repeat that the doctrine of the Causation of human actions, improperly called the doctrine of Necessity, affirms no mysterious *nexus* or overruling fatality: it asserts only that men's actions are the joint result of the general laws and circumstances of human nature, and of their own particular characters, those characters again being the consequence of the natural and artificial circumstances that constituted their education, among which circumstances must be reckoned their own conscious efforts. Any one who is willing to take (if the expression may be permitted) the trouble of thinking himself into the doctrine as thus stated, will find it, I believe, not only a faithful interpretation of the universal experience of human conduct, but a correct representation of the mode in which he himself, in every particular case, spontaneously interprets his own experience of that conduct.

But if this principle is true of individual man, it must be true of collective man. If it is the law of human life, the law must be realised in history. The experience of human affairs when looked at *en masse*, must be in accordance with it if true, or repugnant to it if false. The support which this *à posteriori* verification affords to the law is the part of the case which has been most clearly and triumphantly brought out by Mr Buckle.

The facts of statistics, since they have been made a subject of careful recordation and study, have yielded conclusions, some of which have been very startling to persons not accustomed to regard moral actions as subject to uniform laws. The very events which in their own nature appear most capricious and uncertain, and which in any individual case no attainable degree of knowledge would enable us to foresee, occur, when considerable numbers are taken into the account, with a degree of regularity approaching to mathematical. What act is there which all would consider as more completely dependent on individual character, and on the exercise of individual free will, than that of slaying a fellow-creature? Yet in any large country, the number of murders, in proportion to the population, varies (it has been found) very little from one year to another, and in its variations never deviates widely from a certain average. What is still more remarkable, there is a similar approach to constancy in the proportion of these murders annually committed with every particular kind of instrument. There is a like approximation to identity, as between one year ·and another, in the comparative number of legitimate and of illegitimate births. The same thing is found true of suicides, accidents, and all other social phenomena of which the registration is sufficiently perfect; one of the most curiously illustrative examples being the fact, ascertained by the register of the London and Paris post-offices, that the number of letters posted which the writers have forgotten to direct is nearly the same, in proportion to the whole number of letters posted, in one year, as in another. 'Year after year,' says Mr Buckle, 'the same proportion of letter-writers forget this simple act, so that for each successive period we can actually foretell the number of persons whose memory will fail them in regard to this trifling, and, as it might appear, accidental occurrence.'*

This singular degree of regularity *en masse*, combined with the extreme of irregularity in the cases composing the mass, is a felicitous verification *à posteriori* of the law of causation in its application to human conduct. Assuming the truth of that law, every human action, every murder, for instance, is the concurrent result of two sets of causes. On the one part, the general circumstances of the country and its inhabitants; the moral, educational, economical, and other influences operating on the whole people, and constituting what we term the state of civilisation. On the other part, the great variety of influences special to the individual: his temperament, and other peculiarities of organisation, his parentage, habitual associates, temptations, and so forth. If we now take the whole of the instances which occur within a sufficiently large field to exhaust all the combinations of these special influences, or, in other words, to eliminate chance; and if all these instances have occurred within such narrow limits of time that no material change can have taken

* *History of Civilisation* i. 30.

place in the general influences constituting the state of civilisation of the country, we may be certain that if human actions are governed by invariable laws, the aggregate result will be something like a constant quantity. The number of murders committed within that space and time being the effect partly of general causes which have not varied, and partly of partial causes the whole round of whose variations has been included, will be, practically speaking, invariable.

Literally and mathematically invariable it is not, and could not be expected to be; because the period of a year is too short to include *all* the possible combinations of partial causes, while it is, at the same time, sufficiently long to make it probable that in some years, at least, of every series, there will have been introduced new influences of a more or less general character; such as a more vigorous or a more relaxed police; some temporary excitement from political or religious causes; or some incident generally notorious, of a nature to act morbidly on the imagination. That in spite of these unavoidable imperfections in the data, there should be so very trifling a margin of variation in the annual results, is a brilliant confirmation of the general theory.

2. *It does not imply the insignificance of moral causes*

The same considerations which thus strikingly corroborate the evidence of the doctrine that historical facts are the invariable effects of causes, tend equally to clear that doctrine from various misapprehensions, the existence of which has been put in evidence by the recent discussions. Some persons, for instance, seemingly imagine the doctrine to imply, not merely that the total number of murders committed in a given space and time is entirely the effect of the general circumstances of society, but that every particular murder is so too; that the individual murderer is, so to speak, a mere instrument in the hands of general causes; that he himself has no option, or, if he has, and chose to exercise it, some one else would be necessitated to take his place; that if any one of the actual murderers had abstained from the crime, some person who would otherwise have remained innocent would have committed an extra murder to make up the average. Such a corollary would certainly convict any theory which necessarily led to it of absurdity. It is obvious, however, that each particular murder depends, not on the general state of society only, but on that combined with causes special to the case, which are generally much more powerful; and if these special causes, which have greater influence than the general ones in causing every particular murder, have no influence on the number of murders in a given period, it is because the field of observation is so extensive as to include all possible combinations of the special causes – all varieties of individual character and individual temptation compatible with the general state of society. The collective experiment, as it may be termed, exactly separates the effect of the general from that of the special causes, and shows the net result of the former; but it declares nothing at all respecting the amount of influence of the special causes, be it greater or smaller, since the scale of the experiment extends to the number of cases within which the effects of the special causes balance one another, and disappear in that of the general causes.

I will not pretend that all the defenders of the theory have always kept their language free from this same confusion, and have shown no tendency to exalt the influence of general causes at the expense of special. I am of opinion, on the contrary, that they have done so in a very great degree, and by so doing have encumbered their theory with difficulties, and laid it open to objections which do not necessarily affect it. Some, for example, (among whom is Mr Buckle himself,) have inferred, or allowed it to be supposed that they inferred, from the regularity in the recurrence of events which depend on moral qualities, that the moral qualities of mankind are little capable of being improved, or are of little importance in the general progress of society, compared with intellectual or economic causes. But to draw this inference is to forget that the statistical tables from which the invariable averages are deduced were compiled from facts occurring within narrow geographical limits, and in a small number of successive years; that is, from a field the whole of which was under the operation of the same general causes, and during too short a time to allow of much change therein. All moral causes but those common to the country generally have been eliminated by the great number of instances taken; and those which are common to the whole country have not varied considerably in the short space of time comprised in the observations. If we admit the supposition that they have varied; if we compare one age with another, or one country with another, or even one part of a country with another, differing in position and character as to the moral elements, the crimes committed within a year give no longer the same, but a widely different numerical aggregate. And this cannot but be the case; for inasmuch as every single crime committed by an individual mainly depends on his moral qualities, the crimes committed by the entire population of the country must depend in an equal degree on their collective moral qualities. To render this element inoperative upon the large scale it would be necessary to suppose that the general moral average of mankind does not vary from country to country, or from age to age; which is not true, and even if it were true, could not possibly be proved by any existing statistics. I do not on this account the less agree in the opinion of Mr Buckle, that the intellectual element in mankind, including in that expression the nature of their beliefs, the amount of their knowledge, and the development of their intelligence, is the predominant circumstance in determining their progress. But I am of this opinion, not because I regard their moral or economical condition either as less powerful or less variable agencies, but because these are in a great degree the consequences of the intellectual condition, and are, in all cases, limited by it, as was observed in the preceding chapter. The intellectual changes are the most conspicuous agents in history, not from their superior force, considered in themselves, but because practically they work with the united power belonging to all three.*

* I have been assured by an intimate friend of Mr Buckle that he would not have withheld his assent from these remarks, and that he never intended to affirm or imply that mankind are not progressive in their moral as well as in their intellectual qualities. 'In dealing with his problem, he availed himself of the artifice resorted to by the Political Economist, who leaves out of consideration the generous and benevolent sentiments, and founds his science on the proposition that mankind are actuated by acquisitive propensities alone', not because such is the fact, but because it is necessary to begin by treating the principal influence as if it was the sole one, and make the due corrections afterwards. 'He desired to make abstraction of the intellect as the determining and dynamical element of the progression, eliminating the more dependent set of conditions, and treating the more active one as if it were an entirely independent variable.'

The same friend of Mr Buckle states that when he used expressions which seemed to exaggerate the influence of general at the expense of special causes, and especially at the expense of the influence of individual minds, Mr Buckle really intended no more than to affirm emphatically that the greatest men cannot effect great changes in human affairs unless the general mind has been in some considerable degree prepared for them by the general circumstances of the age; a truth which, of course, no one thinks of denying. And there certainly are passages in Mr Buckle's writings which speak of the influence exercised by great individual intellects in as strong terms as could be desired.

3. Nor does it imply the inefficacy of the characters of individuals and of the acts of government

There is another distinction often neglected in the discussion of this subject, which it is extremely important to observe. The theory of the subjection of social progress to invariable laws is often held in conjunction with the doctrine that social progress cannot be materially influenced by the exertions of individual persons or by the acts of governments. But though these opinions are often held by the same persons, they are two very different opinions, and the confusion between them is the eternally recurring error of confounding Causation with Fatalism. Because whatever happens will be the effect of causes, human volitions among the rest, it does not follow that volitions, even those of peculiar individuals, are not of great efficacy as causes. If any one in a storm at sea, because about the same number of persons in every year perish by shipwreck, should conclude that it was useless for him to attempt to save his own life, we should call him a Fatalist, and should remind him that the efforts of shipwrecked persons to save their lives are so far from being immaterial, that the average amount of those efforts is one of the causes on which the ascertained annual number of deaths by shipwreck depend. However universal the laws of social development may be, they cannot be more universal or more rigorous than those of the physical agencies of nature; yet human will can convert these into instruments of its designs, and the extent to which it does so makes the chief difference between savages and the most highly civilised people. Human and social facts, from their more complicated nature, are not less, but more, modifiable than mechanical and chemical facts; human agency, therefore, has still greater power over them. And accordingly, those who maintain that the evolution of society depends exclusively, or almost exclusively, on general causes, always include among these the collective knowledge and intellectual development of the race. But if of the race, why not also of some powerful monarch or thinker, or of the ruling portion of some political society, acting through its government? Though the varieties of character among ordinary individuals neutralise one another on any large scale, exceptional individuals in important positions do not in any given age neutralise one another; there was not another Themistocles, or Luther, or Julius Caesar, of equal powers and contrary dispositions, who exactly balanced the given Themistocles, Luther, and Caesar, and prevented them from having any permanent effect. Moreover, for aught that appears, the volitions of exceptional persons, or the opinions and purposes of the individuals who at some particular time compose a government, may be indispensable links in the chain of causation by which even the general causes produce their effects; and I believe this to be the only tenable form of the theory.

Lord Macaulay, in a celebrated passage of one of his early essays (let me add that it was one which he did not himself choose to reprint) gives expression to the doctrine of the absolute inoperativeness of great men, more unqualified, I should think, than has been given to it by any writer of equal abilities. He compares them to persons who merely stand on a loftier height, and thence receive the sun's rays a little earlier than the rest of the human race:

> The sun illuminates the hills while it is still below the horizon, and truth is discovered by the highest minds a little before it becomes manifest to the multitude. This is the extent of their superiority. They are the first to catch and reflect a light which, without their assistance, must in a short time be visible to those who lie far beneath them.*

If this metaphor is to be carried out, it follows that if there had been no Newton the world would not only have had the Newtonian system, but would have had it equally soon, as the sun would have risen just as early to spectators in the plain if there had been no mountain at hand to catch still earlier rays. And so it would be if truths, like the sun, rose by their own proper motion, without human effort, but not otherwise. I believe that if Newton had not lived, the world must have waited for the Newtonian philosophy until there had been another Newton or his equivalent. No ordinary man, and no succession of ordinary men, could have achieved it. I will not go the length of saying that what Newton did in a single life might not have been done in successive steps by some of those who followed him, each singly inferior to him in genius. But even the least of those steps required a man of great intellectual superiority. Eminent men do not merely see the coming light from the hill-top; they mount on the

* Essay on Dryden, in *Miscellaneous Writings* i. 186.

hill-top and evoke it; and if no one had ever ascended thither, the light, in many cases, might never have risen upon the plain at all. Philosophy and religion are abundantly amenable to general causes; yet few will doubt that had there been no Socrates, no Plato, and no Aristotle, there would have been no philosophy for the next two thousand years, nor in all probability then; and that if there had been no Christ and no St. Paul, there would have been no Christianity.

The point in which, above all, the influence of remarkable individuals is decisive, is in determining the celerity of the movement. In most states of society it is the existence of great men which decides even whether there shall be any progress. It is conceivable that Greece, or that Christian Europe, might have been progressive in certain periods of their history through general causes only; but if there had been no Mahomet, would Arabia have produced Avicenna or Averroes, or Caliphs of Bagdad or of Cordova? In determining, however, in what manner and order the progress of mankind shall take place, if it take place at all, much less depends on the character of individuals. There is a sort of necessity established in this respect by the general laws of human nature, by the constitution of the human mind. Certain truths cannot be discovered or inventions made unless certain others have been made first; certain social improvements, from the nature of the case, can only follow, and not precede, others. The order of human progress, therefore, may to a certain extent have definite laws assigned to it; while as to its celerity, or even as to its taking place at all, no generalisation, extending to the human species generally, can possibly be made, but only some very precarious approximate generalisations, confined to the small portion of mankind in whom there has been anything like consecutive progress within the historical period, and deduced from their special position, or collected from their particular history. Even looking to the *manner* of progress, the order of succession of social states, there is need of great flexibility in our generalisations. The limits of variation in the possible development of social, as of animal life, are a subject of which little is yet understood, and are one of the great problems in social science. It is, at all events, a fact that different portions of mankind, under the influence of different circumstances, have developed themselves in a more or less different manner and into different forms; and among these determining circumstances, the individual character of their great speculative thinkers or practical organisers may well have been one. Who can tell how profoundly the whole subsequent history of China may have been influenced by the individuality of Confucius? and of Sparta (and hence of Greece and the world) by that of Lycurgus?

Concerning the nature and extent of what a great man under favourable circumstances can do for mankind, as well as of what a government can do for a nation, many different opinions are possible; and every shade of opinion on these points is consistent with the fullest recognition that there are invariable laws of historical phenomena. Of course the degree of influence which has to be assigned to these more special agencies makes a great difference in the precision which can be given to the general laws, and in the confidence with which predictions can be grounded on them. Whatever depends on the peculiarities of individuals, combined with the accident of the positions they hold, is necessarily incapable of being foreseen. Undoubtedly, these casual combinations might be eliminated like any others by taking a sufficiently large cycle: the peculiarities of a great historical character make their influence felt in history sometimes for several thousand years, but it is highly probable that they will make no difference at all at the end of fifty millions. Since, however, we cannot obtain an average of the vast length of time necessary to exhaust all the possible combinations of great men and circumstances, as much of the law of evolution of human affairs as depends upon this average is and remains inaccessible to us; and within the next thousand years, which are of considerably more importance to us than the whole remainder of the fifty millions, the favourable and unfavourable combinations which will occur will be to us purely accidental. We cannot foresee the advent of great men. Those who introduce new speculative thoughts or great practical conceptions into the world cannot have their epoch fixed beforehand. What science can do is this. It can trace through past history the general causes which had brought mankind into that preliminary state, which, when the right sort of great man appeared, rendered them accessible to his influence. If this state continues, experience renders it tolerably certain that in a longer or shorter period the great man will be produced, provided that the general circumstances of the country and people are (which very often they are not) compatible with his existence; of which point also science can in some measure judge. It is in this manner that the results of progress, except as to the celerity of their production, can be, to a certain extent, reduced to regularity and law. And the belief that they can be so is equally consistent with assigning very great, or very little efficacy, to the influence of exceptional men, or of the acts of governments. And the same may be said of all other accidents and disturbing causes.

4. *The historical importance of eminent men and of the policy of governments illustrated*

It would nevertheless be a great error to assign only a trifling importance to the agency of eminent individuals, or of governments. It must not be concluded that the influence of either is small because they cannot bestow what the general circumstances of society, and the course of its previous history, have not prepared it to receive. Neither thinkers nor governments effect all that they intend, but in compensation they often produce important results which they did not in the least foresee. Great men and great actions are seldom wasted: they send forth a thousand unseen influences, more effective than those which are seen; and though nine out of every ten things done, with a good purpose, by those who are in advance of their age, produce no material effect, the tenth thing produces effects twenty times as great as any one would have dreamed of predicting from it. Even the men who for want of sufficiently favourable circumstances left no impress at all upon their own age have often been of the greatest value to posterity. Who could appear to have lived more entirely in vain than some of the early heretics? They were burnt or massacred, their writings extirpated, their memory anathematised, and their very names and existence left for seven or eight centuries in the obscurity of musty manuscripts – their history to be gathered, perhaps, only from the sentences by which they were condemned. Yet the memory of these men – men who resisted certain pretensions or certain dogmas of the Church in the very age in which the unanimous assent of Christendom was afterwards claimed as having been given to them, and asserted as the ground of their authority – broke the chain of tradition, established a series of precedents for resistance, inspired later Reformers with the courage, and armed them with the weapons, which they needed when mankind were better prepared to follow their impulse. To this example from men let us add another from governments. The comparatively enlightened rule of which Spain had the benefit during a considerable part of the eighteenth century did not correct the fundamental defects of the Spanish people; and in consequence, though it did great temporary good, so much of that good perished with it, that it may plausibly be affirmed to have had no permanent effect. The case has been cited as a proof how little governments can do in opposition to the causes which have determined the general character of the nation. It does show how much there is which they cannot do; but not that they can do nothing. Compare what Spain was at the beginning of that half century of liberal government with what she had become at its close. That period fairly let in the light of European thought upon the more educated classes, and it never afterwards ceased to go on spreading. Previous to that time the change was in an inverse direction; culture, light, intellectual, and even material activity, were becoming extinguished. Was it nothing to arrest this downward and convert it into an upward course? How much that Charles the Third and Aranda could not do has been the ultimate consequence of what they did! To that half century Spain owes that she has got rid of the Inquisition, that she has got rid of the monks, that she now has parliaments and (save in exceptional intervals) a free press, and the feelings of freedom and citizenship, and is acquiring railroads and all the other constituents of material and economical progress. In the Spain which preceded that era, there was not a single element at work which could have led to these results in any length of time, if the country had continued to be governed as it was by the last princes of the Austrian dynasty, or if the Bourbon rulers had been from the first what, both in Spain and in Naples, they afterwards became.

And if a government can do much, even when it seems to have done little, in causing positive improvement, still greater are the issues dependent on it in the way of warding off evils, both internal and external, which else would stop improvement altogether. A good or a bad counsellor, in a single city at a particular crisis, has affected the whole subsequent fate of the world. It is as certain as any contingent judgment respecting historical events can be, that if there had been no Themistocles there would have been no victory of

Salamis; and had there not, where would have been all our civilisation? How different again would have been the issue if Epaminondas or Timoleon, or even Iphicrates, instead of Chares and Lysicles, had commanded at Chaeroneia. As is well said in the second of two essays on the Study of History* – in my judgment the soundest and most philosophical productions which the recent controversies on this subject have called forth – historical science authorises not absolute, but only conditional predictions. General causes count for much, but individuals also 'produce great changes in history, and colour its whole complexion long after their death. ... No one can doubt that the Roman republic would have subsided into a military despotism if Julius Caesar had never lived'; (thus much was rendered practically certain by general causes;) 'but is it at all clear that in that case Gaul would ever have formed a province of the empire? Might not Varus have lost his three legions on the banks of the Rhone? and might not that river have become the frontier instead of the Rhine? This might well have happened if Caesar and Crassus had changed provinces; and it is surely impossible to say that in such an event the venue (as lawyers say) of European civilisation might not have been changed. The Norman Conquest in the same way was as much the act of a single man as the writing of a newspaper article; and knowing as we do the history of that man and his family, we can retrospectively predict with all but infallible certainty that no other person' (no other in that age, I presume, is meant) 'could have accomplished the enterprise. If it had not been accomplished, is there any ground to suppose that either our history or our national character would have been what they are?'

As is most truly remarked by the same writer, the whole stream of Grecian history, as cleared up by Mr Grote, is one series of examples how often events on which the whole destiny of subsequent civilisation turned were dependent on the personal character for good or evil of some one individual. It must be said, however, that Greece furnishes the most extreme example of this nature to be found in history, and is a very exaggerated specimen of the general tendency. It has happened only that once, and will probably never happen again, that the fortunes of mankind depended upon keeping a certain order of things in existence in a single town, or a country scarcely

* In the *Cornhill Magazine* for June and July 1861.

larger than Yorkshire; capable of being ruined or saved by a hundred causes, of very slight magnitude in comparison with the general tendencies of human affairs. Neither ordinary accidents nor the characters of individuals can ever again be so vitally important as they then were. The longer our species lasts and the more civilised it becomes, the more, as Comte remarks, does the influence of past generations over the present, and of mankind *en masse* over every individual in it, predominate over other forces: and though the course of affairs never ceases to be susceptible of alteration both by accidents and by personal qualities, the increasing preponderance of the collective agency of the species over all minor causes is constantly bringing the general evolution of the race into something which deviates less from a certain and preappointed track. Historical science, therefore, is always becoming more possible; not solely because it is better studied, but because, in every generation, it becomes better adapted for study.

CHAPTER TWELVE

Of the Logic of Practice, or Art; including Morality and Policy

1. Morality not a science, but an art

In the preceding chapters we have endeavoured to characterise the present state of those among the branches of knowledge called Moral which are sciences in the only proper sense of the term, that is, inquiries into the course of nature. It is customary, however, to include under the term Moral Knowledge, and even (though improperly) under that of Moral Science, an inquiry the results of which do not express themselves in the indicative, but in the imperative mood, or in periphrases equivalent to it; what is called the knowledge of duties, practical ethics, or morality.

Now, the imperative mood is the characteristic of art, as distinguished from science. Whatever speaks in rules or precepts, not in assertions respecting matters of fact, is art; and ethics or morality is properly a portion of the art corresponding to the sciences of human nature and society. *

The Method, therefore, of Ethics, can be no other than that of Art, or Practice, in general: and the portion yet uncompleted, of the task which we proposed to ourselves in the concluding Book is to characterise the general Method of Art, as distinguished from Science.

2. Relations between rules of art and the theorems of the corresponding science

In all branches of practical business, there are cases in which

---

* It is almost superfluous to observe, that there is another meaning of the word Art, in which it may be said to denote the poetical department or aspect of things in general, in contradistinction to the scientific. In the text, the word is used in its older, and, I hope, not yet obsolete sense.

individuals are bound to conform their practice to a pre-established rule, while there are others in which it is part of their task to find or construct the rule by which they are to govern their conduct. The first, for example, is the case of a judge under a definite written code. The judge is not called upon to determine what course would be intrinsically the most advisable in the particular case in hand, but only within what rule of law it falls; what the legislature has ordained to be done in the kind of case, and must therefore be presumed to have intended in the individual case. The method must here be wholly and exclusively one of ratiocination or syllogism; and the process is obviously what in our analysis of the syllogism we showed that all ratiocination is, namely, the interpretation of a formula.

In order that our illustration of the opposite case may be taken from the same class of subjects as the former, we will suppose, in contrast with the situation of the judge, the position of the legislator. As the judge has laws for his guidance, so the legislator has rules and maxims of policy; but it would be a manifest error to suppose that the legislator is bound by these maxims in the same manner as the judge is bound by the laws, and that all he has to do is to argue down from them to the particular case, as the judge does from the laws. The legislator is bound to take into consideration the reasons or grounds of the maxim; the judge has nothing to do with those of the law, except so far as a consideration of them may throw light upon the intention of the lawmaker, where his words have left it doubtful. To the judge, the rule, once positively ascertained, is final: but the legislator, or other practitioner, who goes by rules rather than by their reasons, like the old-fashioned German tacticians who were vanquished by Napoleon, or the physician who preferred that his patients should die by rule rather than recover contrary to it, is rightly judged to be a mere pedant, and the slave of his formulas.

Now, the reasons of a maxim of policy, or of any other rule of art, can be no other than the theorems of the corresponding science.

The relation in which rules of art stand to doctrines of science may be thus characterised. The art proposes to itself an end to be attained, defines the end, and hands it over to the science. The science receives it, considers it as a phenomenon or effect to be studied, and having investigated its causes and conditions, sends it back to art with a theorem of the combination of circumstances by which it could be produced. Art then examines these combinations of circumstances, and according as any of them are or are not in human power, pronounces the end attainable or not. The only one of the premises, therefore, which Art supplies is the original major premise, which asserts that the attainment of the given end is desirable. Science then lends to Art the proposition (obtained by a series of inductions or of deductions) that the performance of certain actions will attain the end. From these premises Art concludes that the performance of these actions is desirable, and finding it also practicable, converts the theorem into a rule or precept.

3. What is the proper function of rules of art?

It deserves particular notice that the theorem or speculative truth is not ripe for being turned into a precept until the whole, and not a part merely, of the operation which belongs to science has been performed. Suppose that we have completed the scientific process only up to a certain point; have discovered that a particular cause will produce the desired effect, but have not ascertained all the negative conditions which are necessary, that is, all the circumstances which, if present, would prevent its production. If, in this imperfect state of the scientific theory, we attempt to frame a rule of art, we perform that operation prematurely. Whenever any counteracting cause, overlooked by the theorem, takes place, the rule will be at fault; we shall employ the means, and the end will not follow. No arguing from or about the rule itself will then help us through the difficulty; there is nothing for it but to turn back and finish the scientific process which should have preceded the formation of the rule. We must reopen the investigation to inquire into the remainder of the conditions on which the effect depends; and only after we have ascertained the whole of these are we prepared to transform the completed law of the effect into a precept, in which those circumstances or combinations of circumstances which the science exhibits as conditions are prescribed as means.

It is true that, for the sake of convenience, rules must be formed from something less than this ideally perfect theory; in the first place, because the theory can seldom be made ideally perfect; and next, because, if all the counteracting contingencies, whether of frequent or of rare occurrence, were included, the rules would be too cumbrous to be apprehended and remembered by ordinary capacities, on the common occasions of life. The rules of art do not attempt to comprise more conditions than require to be attended to in ordinary cases; and are therefore always imperfect. In the manual arts, where the requisite conditions are not numerous, and where those which the rules do not specify are generally either plain to common observation or speedily learnt from practice, rules may often be safely acted on by persons who know nothing more than the rule. But in the complicated affairs of life, and still more in those of states and societies, rules cannot be relied on, without constantly referring back to the scientific laws on which they are founded. To know what are the practical contingencies which require a modification of the rule, or which are altogether exceptions to it, is to know what combinations of circumstances would interfere with, or entirely counteract, the consequences of those laws: and this can only be learnt by a reference to the theoretic grounds of the rule.

By a wise practitioner, therefore, rules of conduct will only be considered as provisional. Being made for the most numerous cases, or for those of most ordinary occurrence, they point out the manner in which it will be least perilous to act, where time or means do not exist for analysing the actual circumstances of the case, or where we cannot trust our judgment in estimating them. But they do not at all supersede the propriety of going through (when circumstances permit) the scientific process requisite for framing a rule from the data of the particular case before us. At the same time, the common rule may very properly serve as an admonition that a certain mode of action has been found by ourselves and others to be well adapted to the cases of most common occurrence; so that if it be unsuitable to the case in hand, the reason of its being so will be likely to arise from some unusual circumstance.

4. Art cannot be deductive

The error is therefore apparent of those who would deduce the line of conduct proper to particular cases from supposed universal practical maxims, overlooking the necessity of constantly referring back to the principles of the speculative science, in order to be sure of attaining even the specific end which the rules have in view. How much greater still, then, must the error be of setting up such unbending principles, not merely as universal rules for attaining a given end, but as rules of conduct generally; without regard to the possibility, not only that some modifying cause may prevent the attainment of the given end by the means which the rule prescribes, but that success itself may conflict with some other end, which may possibly chance to be more desirable.

This is the habitual error of many of the political speculators whom I have characterised as the geometrical school; especially in France, where ratiocination from rules of practice forms the staple commodity of journalism and political oratory; a misapprehension of the functions of Deduction which has brought much discredit, in the estimation of other countries, upon the spirit of generalisation so honourably characteristic of the French mind. The common-places of politics, in France, are large and sweeping practical maxims, from which, as ultimate premises, men reason downwards to particular applications, and this they call being logical and consistent. For instance, they are perpetually arguing that such and such a measure ought to be adopted, because it is a consequence of the principle on which the form of government is founded; of the principle of legitimacy, or the principle of the sovereignty of the people. To which it may be answered, that if these be really practical principles, they must rest on speculative grounds; the sovereignty of the people (for example) must be a right foundation for government, because a government thus constituted tends to produce certain beneficial effects. Inasmuch, however, as no government produces all possible beneficial effects, but all are attended with more or fewer inconveniences, and since these cannot usually be combated by means drawn from the very causes which produce them, it would be often a much stronger recommendation of some practical arrangement that it does not follow from what is called the general principle of the government, than that it does. Under a government of legitimacy, the presumption is far rather in favour of institutions of popular origin; and in a democracy, in favour of arrangements tending to check the impetus of popular will. The line of argumentation so commonly mistaken in France for political philosophy tends to the practical conclusion that we should exert our utmost efforts to aggravate, instead of alleviating, whatever are the characteristic imperfections of the system of institutions which we prefer, or under which we happen to live.

5. *Every art consists of truths of science, arranged in the order suitable for some practical use*

The grounds, then, of every rule of art are to be found in theorems of science. An art, or a body of art, consists of the rules, together with as much of the speculative propositions as comprises the justification of those rules. The complete art of any matter includes a selection of such a portion from the science as is necessary to show on what conditions the effects which the art aims at producing depend. And Art in general consists of the truths of science, arranged in the most convenient order for practice, instead of the order which is the most convenient for thought. Science groups and arranges its truths so as to enable us to take in at one view as much as possible of the general order of the universe. Art, though it must assume the same general laws, follows them only into such of their detailed consequences as have led to the formation of rules of conduct, and brings together from parts of the field of science most remote from one another the truths relating to the production of the different and heterogeneous conditions necessary to each effect which the exigencies of practical life require to be produced.*

Science, therefore, following one cause to its various effects, while art traces one effect to its multiplied and diversified causes and conditions, there is need of a set of intermediate scientific truths, derived from the higher generalities of science, and destined to serve as the generalia or first principles of the various arts. The scientific operation of framing these intermediate principles, M. Comte characterises as one of those results of philosophy which are reserved for futurity. The only complete example which he points out as actually realised, and which can be held up as a type to be imitated in more important matters, is the general theory of the art of Descriptive Geometry, as conceived by M. Monge. It is not, however, difficult to understand what the nature of these intermediate principles must generally be. After framing the most comprehensive possible conception of the end to be aimed at, that is, of the effect to be produced, and determining in the same comprehensive manner the set of conditions on which that effect depends, there remains to be taken a general survey of the resources which can be commanded for

---

* Professor Bain and others call the selection from the truths of science made for the purposes of an art, a Practical Science; and confine the name Art to the actual rules.

realising this set of conditions; and when the result of this survey has been embodied in the fewest and most extensive propositions possible, those propositions will express the general relation between the available means and the end, and will constitute the general scientific theory of the art, from which its practical methods will follow as corollaries.

6. *Teleology, or the doctrine of ends*

But though the reasonings which connect the end or purpose of every art with its means belong to the domain of Science, the definition of the end itself belongs exclusively to Art, and forms its peculiar province. Every art has one first principle, or general major premise, not borrowed from science; that which enunciates the object aimed at, and affirms it to be a desirable object. The builder's art assumes that it is desirable to have buildings; architecture (as one of the fine arts) that it is desirable to have them beautiful or imposing. The hygienic and medical arts assume, the one that the preservation of health, the other that the cure of disease, are fitting and desirable ends. These are not propositions of science. Propositions of science assert a matter of fact: an existence, a co-existence, a succession, or a resemblance. The propositions now spoken of do not assert that anything is, but enjoin or recommend that something should be. They are a class by themselves. A proposition of which the predicate is expressed by the words *ought* or *should he*, is generically different from one which is expressed by *is* or *will be*. It is true that, in the largest sense of the words, even these propositions assert something as a matter of fact. The fact affirmed in them is, that the conduct recommended excites in the speaker's mind the feeling of approbation. This, however, does not go to the bottom of the matter, for the speaker's approbation is no sufficient reason why other people should approve; nor ought it to be a conclusive reason even with himself. For the purposes of practice, every one must be required to justify his approbation; and for this there is need of general premises, determining what are the proper objects of approbation, and what the proper order of precedence among those objects.

These general premises, together with the principal conclusions which may be deduced from them, form (or rather might form) a body of doctrine, which is properly the Art of Life, in its three departments, Morality, Prudence or Policy, and Aesthetics; the Right, the Expedient, and the Beautiful or Noble, in human conduct and works. To this art (which, in the main, is unfortunately still to be created) all other arts are subordinate; since its principles are those which must determine whether the special aim of any particular art is worthy and desirable, and what is its place in the scale of desirable things. Every art is thus a joint result of laws of nature disclosed by science, and of the general principles of what has been called Teleology, or the Doctrine of Ends;* which, borrowing the language of the German metaphysicians, may also be termed, not improperly, the principles of Practical Reason.

A scientific observer or reasoner, merely as such, is not an adviser for practice. His part is only to show that certain consequences follow from certain causes, and that to obtain certain ends, certain means are the most effectual. Whether the ends themselves are such as ought to be pursued, and if so, in what cases and to how great a length, it is no part of his business as a cultivator of science to decide, and science alone will never qualify him for the decision. In purely physical science there is not much temptation to assume this ulterior office; but those who treat of human nature and society invariably claim it; they always undertake to say, not merely what is, but what ought to be. To entitle them to do this, a complete doctrine of Teleology is indispensable. A scientific theory, however perfect, of the subject-matter, considered merely as part of the order of nature, can in no degree serve as a substitute. In this respect the various subordinate arts afford a misleading analogy. In them there is seldom any visible necessity for justifying the end, since in general its desirableness is denied by nobody, and it is only when the question of precedence is to be decided between that end and some other, that the general principles of Teleology have to be called in; but a writer on Morals and Politics requires those principles at every step. The most elaborate and well-digested exposition of the laws of succession and co-existence among mental or social phenomena, and of their relation to one another as causes and effects, will be of no avail towards the art of Life or of Society, if the ends to be aimed at by

---

* The word Teleology is also, but inconveniently and improperly, employed by some writers as a name for the attempt to explain the phenomena of the universe from final causes.

that art are left to the vague suggestions of the *intellectus sibi permissus*, or are taken for granted without analysis or questioning.

7. Necessity of an ultimate standard, or first principle of teleology

There is, then, a *Philosophia Prima* peculiar to Art, as there is one which belongs to Science. There are not only first principles of Knowledge, but first principles of Conduct. There must be some standard by which to determine the goodness or badness, absolute and comparative, of ends or objects of desire. And whatever that standard is, there can be but one: for if there were several ultimate principles of conduct, the same conduct might be approved by one of those principles and condemned by another; and there would be needed some more general principle as umpire between them.

Accordingly, writers on moral philosophy have mostly felt the necessity not only of referring all rules of conduct, and all judgments of praise and blame, to principles, but of referring them to some one principle; some rule or standard, with which all other rules of conduct were required to be consistent, and from which by ultimate consequence they could all be deduced. Those who have dispensed with the assumption of such an universal standard have only been enabled to do so by supposing that a moral sense, or instinct, inherent in our constitution, informs us, both what principles of conduct we are bound to observe, and also in what order these should be subordinated to one another.

The theory of the foundations of morality is a subject which it would be out of place, in a work like this, to discuss at large, and which could not to any useful purpose be treated incidentally. I shall content myself therefore with saying, that the doctrine of intuitive moral principles, even if true, would provide only for that portion of the field of conduct which is properly called moral. For the remainder of the practice of life some general principle, or standard, must still be sought; and if that principle be rightly chosen, it will be found, I apprehend, to serve quite as well for the ultimate principle of Morality, as for that of Prudence, Policy, or Taste.

Without attempting in this place to justify my opinion, or even to define the kind of justification which it admits of, I merely declare my conviction, that the general principle to which all rules of practice ought to conform, and the test by which they should be tried, is that of conduciveness to the happiness of mankind, or rather, of all sentient beings: in other words, that the promotion of happiness is the ultimate principle of Teleology.*

I do not mean to assert that the promotion of happiness should be itself the end of all actions, or even of all rules of action. It is the justification, and ought to be the controller, of all ends, but is not itself the sole end. There are many virtuous actions, and even virtuous modes of action, (though the cases are, I think, less frequent than is often supposed,) by which happiness in the particular instance is sacrificed, more pain being produced than pleasure. But conduct of which this can be truly asserted admits of justification only because it can be shown that on the whole more happiness will exist in the world if feelings are cultivated which will make people, in certain cases, regardless of happiness. I fully admit that this is true: that the cultivation of an ideal nobleness of will and conduct should be to individual human beings an end, to which the specific pursuit either of their own happiness or of that of others (except so far as included in that idea) should, in any case of conflict, give way. But I hold that the very question, what constitutes this elevation of character, is itself to be decided by a reference to happiness as the standard. The character itself should be, to the individual, a paramount end, simply because the existence of this ideal nobleness of character, or of a near approach to it, in any abundance, would go further than all things else towards making human life happy, both in the comparatively humble sense of pleasure and freedom from pain, and in the higher meaning of rendering life, not what it now is almost universally, puerile and insignificant, but such as human beings with highly developed faculties can care to have.

8. Conclusion

With these remarks we must close this summary view of the application of the general logic of scientific inquiry to the moral and social departments of science. Notwithstanding the extreme generality of the principles of method which I have laid down, (a generality which, I trust, is not in this instance synonymous with

---

* For an express discussion and vindication of this principle, see the little volume entitled *Utilitarianism.*

vagueness,) I have indulged the hope that to some of those on whom the task will devolve of bringing those most important of all sciences into a more satisfactory state these observations may be useful, both in removing erroneous and in clearing up the true conceptions of the means by which, on subjects of so high a degree of complication, truth can be attained. Should this hope be realised, what is probably destined to be the great intellectual achievement of the next two or three generations of European thinkers will have been in some degree forwarded.